The Longer Road

A Suite of Poems and Reflections from a Peace Corps Volunteer in Uganda

JOHN TRIMMER

The Longer Road

The road through the woods is stranger
Than if you kept your spot,
Fraught with potential danger,
Filled with painful lot,
But still you may find you'll linger
Because you have been caught,
Not by a vicious finger,
But a peaceful thought.

The road can be full of wonder
If love and life are sought,
Not with a plan to plunder,
Only to be taught,
And so you'll return, no longer
The same to this same spot,
Longer your road, but stronger
You have now been wrought.

CONTENTS

PRELUDE | WHY THIS

Why This

Why this?
Why not something less easy to miss?
Why not words that are more direct,
More like plainspoken text?
Because life is complex,
And so often our logic is vexed
By labyrinths worthy of Daedalus,
Or awe at an opening chrysalis.

Why this?
Why not straightforward sadness or bliss?
Because life often mixes them both,
Spurring us forward to growth.

Why this?
Because life holds mysteriousness:
This thing I did not comprehend
Holds beauty and helps to express
The layers of truth that transcend.

What follows is an attempt to present a journey. It is more a journey of the soul and the mind, rather than a physical one, although it is set during my years of Peace Corps service in Uganda, an experience that took me halfway around the world and back again. It represents the transformation of my own viewpoint – an evolution from a relatively simplistic (and perhaps savior-driven) outlook to one that I think includes greater complexity, humility, respect, and love. The poems and songs contained in these pages were composed either during or soon after my time in Uganda, and the passages of prose that connect them reveal pieces of the life I experienced there. At its core, it is an exploration through the tender underbrush of ideas growing within, guided by people who have become important to me during this episode of my existence.

Before beginning this tale, it occurs to me that offering a bit of background might be useful. As someone who lived in Uganda for only a few years, I certainly cannot deliver a complete explanation of local conditions and cultures. However, perhaps I can provide a few details that will help to set the stage.

Uganda contains fifty-six distinct ethnic groups, brought together by colonial borders. English functions as the national language, but, in many instances, dozens of local languages dominate everyday conversations. When I left the country in 2014, it was estimated that thirty-six million people were living in Uganda, and that figure is growing rapidly. The country's population is one of the fastest growing in the world, and half of its people are fifteen years old or younger.

Like much of the world, Uganda's urban population is increasing quickly, although most people still live in rural areas – in dispersed villages, in small trading centers along major roads, and in regions surrounding larger towns. Especially in these rural areas, many people's lives include some form of small-scale agriculture, in which households grow crops to meet their own needs. If there is any surplus, it might be sold in local markets. Other jobs can be difficult to find and often provide low wages.

A host of conditions can merge to make life difficult for individuals and families. But, despite it all, people's experiences in this place are not a single, sad tale. So much more is there, so much more than I could ever see during the few years I lived and worked in Uganda. The story is considerably more complicated than we might perceive it to be from afar. As with so much in life, joy is mingled with sadness, and the sources of the sadness may not be as simple as we think. Sometimes, I think it can be easy for us to see the difficulties of other places as being straightforward and easily dealt with, if we can just put enough time or money into what we think are obvious solutions. If I have learned nothing else from my experience, I now know that things are often multifaceted and more intricate than they initially appear. They do not always have easy explanations or straightforward answers. How do I handle this ambiguity and complexity within what I encounter?

For a number of reasons, I have always needed a creative, artistic outlet. Throughout much of my life, that outlet has been music. It helps me to release my often restless mind from the overly analytical thoughts and questions that arise from the ambiguities of life, allowing me to begin to respond with sounds that are deeper than words. By the time I was halfway through college, I was playing the cello, the piano, and the guitar almost every day. I was also writing songs and instrumental pieces, many of which explored ideas surrounding spirituality, our place in the world, and the love I saw expressed in the lives of my friends and family.

Unfortunately, during my time in Uganda, many of my life's musical elements were left behind. On the flight over, I was already bringing as much luggage as possible, without adding any large musical instruments. As the months passed, I realized more and more that, faced with one of the most challenging and unfamiliar experiences of my life, I needed another outlet. I think that's why I started writing poetry.

When I had to study it in high school English classes, I remember being less than fond of it. With my analytical mind, I suppose I often found poetry to be too vague or unclear. Over the past few years, however, it has become much more appealing to me. I certainly cannot claim that I now fully comprehend the exact meaning of every poem I read, but I think I understand that accepting a little ambiguity is not necessarily a bad thing. Perhaps, sometimes, poetry can express the transcendence of the universe and the intricacy of our lives more profoundly and acutely than straightforward, explicitly-reasoned prose.

My own poetry, I think, is still in its childhood – supported and guided by the age-old structures of rhythm and rhyme to find expression. But perhaps, in their unpolished youth, the words still have something to say. The poems and songs I have written, springing from and being colored by my experiences in Uganda,

3

attempt to respond to the ambiguity we face and make sense of our place in a world that is so often unjust, unbalanced, and unclear. Their themes focus on what I saw and what I thought as I learned about the people I was living and working with, the physical and spiritual environments that surrounded us, my own evolving understanding of international development work, and the lessons of life and love that blossomed from these encounters.

In the following pages, poems and song lyrics are embedded and interwoven into the story of my Peace Corps service. During training, at the beginning of my time in Uganda, I wrote in a journal every night, and I hoped to continue this practice throughout my service. However, as time went on, as my experience became less like a new, unfamiliar event and felt more like normal life, my devotion to this task waned. Even so, I would intermittently experience stretches of prolific thoughtfulness and journal writing. These contemplative episodes form the framework in which I present my experiences and ideas.

At my relatively young age and insignificant level of experience, it's worth noting that writing about my experiences in this way may involve a certain amount of hubris. Are the events of my life and my thoughts about them really all that important and worthy of dissemination? I tell myself that this work is focused on the lessons of the encounter, on the wisdom of the ages gleaned from my coworkers, my neighbors, and my surroundings, rather than on my own potentially flawed understanding of those events and meetings. And yet, it is all filtered through the lens of my own mind, likely inadequate to the task. But, perhaps, one of the lessons I have learned is that each person's story, and each person's telling of that story, matters and can contribute something to the lives of others.

In the end, I hope this telling says something worthwhile, something valuable for the betterment of the world and of ourselves. If nothing else, it simply constitutes an offering of thanks for the opportunity I have been given – the opportunity to live part of my life in Uganda, to leave part of my heart there, and, in the process, to learn so many things. I offer it now to you. Take from it what you will.

An Offering

First the trouble came inside the living.
Now the issue lives within the telling,
Asking what these memories are giving,
Only once revealed, yet ever swelling,
Overflowing as we go on thinking,
Wondering what fragments lend us meaning,
Fragrant grains of revelation, linking
One unto another, wisdom gleaning.

Sorting through this garden I've been tending,
Filled with seeds remembered from my learning,
In this bulk of fertile thought unending,
Where do I begin my vague discerning?

Is something here, a hidden harmony,
An offering of truth, perhaps unveiled that we might see?

MOVEMENT 1 | ASKING

My Life

My life is not my own to live.
My love is not my own to give.
My life, my love, I owe to all,
Each living thing, be it great or small.

My life is not my own to live.
My love is not my own to give.
If my loss can cause your gain,
Simply help me bear the pain.

My life is not my own to live.
My love is not my own to give.
So wherever you will and wherever you might,
I pray to rise and be a light.

The road stretches out before us as the bus rumbles on, still hours from its destination. Forty-six souls have together begun a journey that will take us much further than John F. Kennedy International Airport in New York City, where the bus will stop. We met yesterday in Philadelphia. Forty-six diverse souls, with varied backgrounds and ideas, united by our newfound status: the August 2011 class of Peace Corps Uganda Trainees, who will be leaving tonight.

We face a long road ahead. After two long flights that will take us to Uganda's Entebbe International Airport, just north of Lake Victoria, we will be spending ten weeks in training, learning local languages, local customs, and technical information that will help us to identify and address local issues. With the completion of training, the true work will begin, as we are sworn in as Peace Corps Volunteers and sent to various sites throughout the country, where we will spend the next two years.

My seat is near the front of the bus on this first leg of a much longer journey. I straighten my back and crane my neck to survey those who are here with me. Some are engaged in soft conversations, learning about the relative strangers sitting near them. Others are dozing, perhaps comfortable and used to the long flights, common frustrations, and semi-controlled frenzy of overseas travel. I find myself in a third group, lost in thought, wondering what lies ahead and what experiences wait in the unknown, slightly apprehensive, perhaps, as I ask myself how I have reached this point. What path has brought me here, moving quickly toward something so new and different?

Why am I speeding down this highway?

Speeding down the Highway

Speeding down the highway, mile after mile,
A thousand trees fly past my eyes, each within its earthen tile,
A hundred houses catch my gaze, only then to fade away,
Lost within the growing distance, shrinking shades of gray.

How many lives do we pass quickly by?
How much existence will never draw nigh,
Never revealing its struggles and secrets?
Only a blur hides the spaces between us.

Do I thunder through the world, scarcely stopping for a smile?
A million details miss my eyes, hidden in each spirit's vial,
Seen by one who simply stays in each moment of today,
Knowing we are tiny pebbles on the universal way.

At some points in my earlier years, I may have been coasting through life. Yes, I worked hard to be a good student, a solid athlete, and a decent musician. But, in my quest to attain certain heights, what did I fly past without even seeing? What life was I not noticing in my somewhat insulated world, growing up in rural, south-central Pennsylvania?

The questions we ask can come to define our lives. We open our minds and release them into the universal ether as we might a butterfly resting in the palm of a hand, hoping, through an unknown combination of our searching and nature's working, we might receive back some form of response. The questions themselves may shed light on new pathways, while any responses that return to us always seem to suggest further avenues of inquiry. If our questions teach us anything, it's that we should never stop learning, never stop searching, never stop yearning for that which eclipses our understanding and goes beyond ourselves.

Slowly, I began to realize that life consisted of more than good grades, winning records, and technical prowess. I was fortunate to have parents who showed me this undeniable truth, even when I was not quite ready to accept it. Through their example, I began to ask more important questions: What can I do to improve the world? What is my role in bettering this place? How can I make an impact?

My father, after every full, grueling day of construction work, drove straight to my grandfather's farm, spending a few hours helping to complete the day's chores, before arriving at home, ready to repeat it all again tomorrow. The question of whether he needed to do all of this, of whether it should be his responsibility, never entered his mind. He worked hard, with unwavering dedication, and continues to do so today. My mother, for as long as I can remember, has spent hours upon hours each week volunteering for the local food bank. At times, it can be frustrating work, but her compassionate and giving heart perseveres to continue serving those who need a helping hand.

I am incredibly fortunate to have known these examples of love, perseverance, and compassion throughout my childhood, and my parents' actions continue to remind me of the questions I constantly need to ask myself: What do I have that could contribute to the world? What can my impact be in improving others' lives?

As college approached, I decided that I would pursue an engineering degree. To be completely honest, music was always my first love, and it continues to be to this day. I had played the cello since elementary school, had been trying to teach myself piano since middle school, and had just begun to compose my first original songs as I finished high school. But, I also enjoyed math and science, and my grades were pretty good. Engineering seemed to me to be a more useful and productive road to pursue, allowing me to have a more practical impact on the world. Although, the specific nature of that impact was not yet apparent.

With this fresh sense of responsibility, undirected as it was, I went off to college. Bucknell University is a small, liberal arts college in Pennsylvania with a good engineering program, and it seemed to be a good fit for me. For one thing, it was still pretty close to my family, and I had never really entertained the possibility that I might find myself somewhere far removed from that family. I expected to move back to the area where I had spent my childhood, find a job, and live out my life, finding some way to have an impact on the local community. I never fashioned myself to be a world traveler. Then, something changed.

At Bucknell, as my thinking became more developed and my perspective began to expand, I found opportunities to learn about and work in other parts of the world, participating in three service trips to Nicaragua. During my senior year, I was part of a team that designed a water supply system for a small village in Suriname. The following summer, using grant funding that we had received, our team helped to build a portion of that system. These short excursions into other countries opened my eyes and profoundly affected my perspective. Although, in total, I had only spent about one and a half months outside of the United States, acute inequalities and other complex issues became unavoidably obvious. In many places on this planet, access to the fundamental necessities of life – clean water, adequate food supplies, shelter, basic education and health care – is not a given. Far from it: many suffer from a severe lack of these essentials, and their lives are constantly at risk because of these unmet needs.

My mind often returns to a scene on the outskirts of Managua, Nicaragua, where I saw hundreds of people living in or near a huge garbage dump, scavenging through the grimy, smoky piles every day for items that might be worth meager sums of money. Young children were there, without shoes to protect their feet from the broken shards of glass on the ground. Teenagers were there, sniffing glue to ease the ever-present pangs of hunger. Without a doubt, the lives of some in this world are drastically harder than others. There is something horribly inhuman about a situation in which people struggle to live, while I have the opportunity to choose the life I want with relative ease.

New, incredibly personal questions began to surface: Why does the location of someone's birth dramatically impact the quality of that person's life? What if I had been born someone else? What if I lived in another place? Can I truly and completely understand life as it is lived by someone else? Certainly, others are not totally defined by the hardships they endure, but those difficulties must play a major role in their lives. I may never know the complete story of another, but perhaps I could at least begin to empathize and work to bring greater justice to this world that I had only begun to discover.

If I Had Been Born Another

Pebbles to skip from sandy point's tip,
Selected by me and my brother,
Light waning fast, while each stone we have cast
Is watched with delight by our mother,
Safe to the last, for a watch unsurpassed
Is kept by the gaze of our father.
Now, can I grip how conditions might flip
If I had been born another?
If I had been born in a faraway country,
My skin shaded differently,
Or just down the street to immigrants, humbly
Working untiringly,
Or if, when I made my original entry
To life, the said pronoun was "she",
What would have changed? How might life's energy
Feel if another I'd be?

Perhaps to find life's key necessities harder,
Perhaps checking rage at the stare of a stranger,
Perhaps, in the night, I would feel greater danger,
Perhaps I might know more of violence and martyr,
Perhaps I would see that I need to go farther

Just to reach some others' point of departure,
Perhaps I'd identify points in the structure
That function as sinkholes for one or another.

Or, perhaps not. Instead, I might find
A similar sketch to my own, first outlined.
The life of the "other", not so foreign, arcane,
Nor embodied completely by hardship and pain,
And yet I won't know all the struggles and triumphs,
What one had to go through, to conquer, to silence.
Always a slice of opacity smothers
The chance to completely feel as another.

Still, we know now what our minds will allow,
Each one is a sister or brother.
Understand that: this place is not flat,
And reach out your hand to another.

Having seen a tiny bit of the injustice and poverty that affects many parts of the world, I knew that something was amiss. Something was out of place. I felt, deep in my soul, that life is out of balance. Beyond the direct impacts of these injustices, all of humanity eventually feels their biting sting, whether we realize it or not. We adversely affect ourselves when others do not have the opportunity to flourish. As I see it, one of the greatest strengths of the human race is its diversity, with numerous cultures, traditions, and philosophies allowing us to see the world through many different lenses. By bringing together various perspectives in cooperation, new and creative options can arise that may be able to lead us forward into a better future. When some of humanity's voices are silenced by poverty, oppression, or injustice, a portion of our collective diversity is lost, at least for a time, and we all suffer from that loss.

With all of these thoughts running through my mind, I felt that I must reach out to lift up those who were suffering, quickly and decisively, for I knew my own nature. This drive, this mindfulness, and this sense of responsibility, as transfixing as they were, also proved to be difficult to sustain. It was so easy to return to the highway of my past and to focus on my own path. From my diversions in the trenches, where the struggle to survive pervaded everything and determined all, I returned to the roads I had traveled for a lifetime, and I settled back into what I had known. In the ever-spinning wheels of my fast-paced life, I inevitably passed by so much of value – so many trees along the road, so many birds soaring in the sky, so many people living out their lives.

Still, I was irrevocably altered by what I had experienced. Although I could return to my previous life, my perception of that life was somehow different. Life's ambiguity and contradiction became much more apparent. Some nights, I would lie awake, struggling with the massively complex structural issues I saw in the world – global poverty and the stifling cycles of discouragement it can create, rampant sickness and disease, the destruction of the precious environment that surrounds us. Other nights, I would quickly fall asleep, easily and peacefully, seemingly content with the state of my life and the lives of those around me.

To some degree, aren't we all creatures of contradiction, and isn't the universe around us filled with contradiction as well? We feel another's touch, but the atoms in our hands may not actually be touching. Each individual is unique, valuable, and significant, and yet we all live on a tiny, insignificant, planetary dot in an obscure section of an incomprehensibly large universe. We can only truly hear the echoes in the depths of the universe, gently suggesting new possibilities, when all is silent…

In Love's Abyss

Step out from beneath the shadows
Of the things you depend upon.
Rise up from safer shallows,
Where comfort leads you on.
"You are more than this," reveals the dawn.
You are more than this…

But still look up from time to time:
The leaves, the birds, the clouds they chase,
Start to realize your size
In still-expanding space.
"A speck to be missed," laughs starlight's face.
A speck to be missed…

"Which view speaks the truth?" you wonder,
As you hover above the shoal.
No paths of stars you've wandered,
But, lighter now, you're whole.
Feel, in love's abyss, your naked soul
Touching all of this...

The contradictions can be maddening, as we try to understand them, to explain them, to cut through them and hollow out a fitting place for ourselves in this complex world. In some ways, the decision to serve in the Peace Corps was an attempt to slice a straight path through the tangle of contradictory thoughts in my mind, to force myself to act. It was a chance to exclaim, "Enough! This world needs a change, and I will be that change. I will live with those who need help, and, as their concerns become my concerns, we will alleviate those concerns together."

Did I, perhaps, answer too quickly? Did I not respect life's complexity? Did I not allow the questions to grow in the asking, transforming into something more than a simple answer? Did I miss the longer road?

With these questions reverberating in my mind, I realize that the bus has slowed to a stop, and my fellow trainees are beginning to collect their bags and move into the airport. Pulled back into the present, I grab my own luggage and follow the crowd. I had forgotten how much I had packed and how heavy and bulky these bags are, but, as we form a line at the baggage check, a small wave of relief washes over me. I would soon be rid of the two largest and weightiest items in my possession.

We slowly make our way through this line, with several of us being asked to redistribute our luggage so that all bags would be under the maximum weight limit. Before I reach the counter, I preemptively relocate some of my own items knowing that my largest bag is very close to the limit. Finally, we all complete the process, and we make our way to the gate. Knowing that we still have a couple of hours before boarding, my mind returns to my previous line of thought, but it doesn't progress much further. Finally, the extended adrenaline rush, caused by the stress of preparing over the past few days and the uncertainty of what is to come, briefly subsides, and my thoughts fade into dreams.

A Sea of Dreams

The dreams, they come less seldom now,
Though memories fade with morning's light.
Fleeting landscapes from worlds unseen,
Partial fragments, pieces of night.

Why these wanderings through the mist,
These brief escapes of fantasy,
Are they, perhaps, designed to hide,
To shield from harsh reality?

Yet how can I deny the cries,
The child, alone, left to die?
Not sure how to dry her eyes,
I find, still, that I must try.

For when this life has passed its prime,
When earthly things seem less sublime,
Will I lament that I was lost
Amid a sea of dreams uncrossed?

Or will I look into your eye,
And say, "I did my best to try,
To sail beyond the fantasy,
To face the true reality."

And still, though oceans separate,
I know you help to navigate.
So as the sun completes its flight,
Let me dream of you tonight.

MOVEMENT 2 | PLUNGING

Contemplative Creation

Contemplative creation from mindful meditation,
Reflective recollections composing new connections.

Consider where you've come from and where you wish to go,
Identify the pathways that cross the chasm where the moments flow,
But at each crossing recognize the newfound chance to improvise,
To free yourself to fly and grow, and set the universe aglow.

Jolted awake by our flight's boarding call, I again follow the group as we begin to board the plane, the voices from my dreams still ringing in my ears. As I find my seat, my mind returns to my previous recollections of motivations and connections that led me to the Peace Corps. Surrounded by others moving in the same direction, I find myself wondering what events and pathways contributed to similar decisions in their lives. From a few short conversations, I've learned that some in our group were originally placed in other countries, and then, in a few cases very suddenly, assignments were altered, and Uganda became their new destination.

Although I think it is different now, when I applied to the Peace Corps, potential volunteers had very little say in the country where they might be placed. A few important things, like previous experience with foreign languages (especially Spanish and French), could make assignments much more likely in countries where those languages were commonly spoken. For the most part, though, country placement was wide open and was dependent upon a long process of medical and administrative clearance. It is a momentous day when a future volunteer discovers the country in which he or she will be serving. I remember receiving a large packet in the mail, with all sorts of information about the country, the current work of volunteers there, and the next steps that must be completed in the process. Immediately, one begins to feel a connection to this place, even though, from a practical standpoint, it may still be totally unknown. I think it takes a special kind of dedication to Peace Corps service when, after the long application and placement process, one's assignment is shifted to a completely different place, perhaps with little warning. In other words, I already have a great deal of respect for those around me, even though I only met them yesterday.

Although I was not faced with a sudden change in placement, my own process of navigating the Peace Corps system was not exactly simple and straightforward. I applied during my senior year at Bucknell and was interviewed that winter. The interview itself seemed to go fairly well, but, at the end, it became evident that I was missing something important. Apparently, any upcoming placements that would fit well with an engineering background also required a high level of Spanish, which I didn't have. Yes, I had spent a few weeks in Nicaragua during those service trips, but translators were always close at hand. In high school, I had studied German, which I enjoyed and thought was a good idea at the time, but which was not helping me at all now that I had turned toward work in the developing world. I did come away from the interview with a possible offer to teach English on one of the Pacific islands – the information didn't get any more detailed than that – but it didn't seem to be a good fit for me, in part because I had no teaching experience.

I found myself faced with a difficult decision. Should I pursue the offer from the Peace Corps? I was certainly not the ideal candidate for a position as an English teacher, but I also knew that I did not want to follow the typical road of an engineering student. I wanted to be a Peace Corps Volunteer, or something very similar. I was fortunate, at the time, to be surrounded by mentors who encouraged me to continue striking out on this path. A professor pointed me toward something called the Peace Corps Master's International program, which combined Peace Corps service with a Master's degree. Very few of these programs existed across the country, especially for environmental engineers, but we found one that seemed to be a good fit at the University of South Florida. I scrambled to learn as much as I could about the program, and then put together my application in the brief time left before the deadline. A couple of months later, I learned that I had been accepted into the program.

The program at the University of South Florida began with one year on campus, during which I took all of the classes required for the degree. Over the following two to three years, I would be expected to complete a full term of Peace Corps service. While serving overseas, I would also be expected to conduct research contributing to a thesis. Through this program, placement in the Peace Corps was made a bit easier for me, as new positions opened up during my year on campus. I also had the benefit of an additional year of preparation, which included classes specifically designed for overseas development work. Would I have been truly ready for Peace Corps service coming straight out of Bucknell? I'm not sure I'm ready now, but I certainly felt better prepared when, about two-thirds of the way through that year in Florida, I learned of my placement to serve as a water, sanitation, and hygiene volunteer in Uganda.

Looking back on this progression, it seems to me that my path to this point has been ideally suited to my aspirations, needs, and motivations. In many instances, it did not proceed as I had expected. Rather, it unfolded in a better way than I could have intended or designed. I don't think I am unique in this realization, but it is also clear that many people face extremely difficult circumstances that are far from perfect. Regardless of how those people respond and navigate the roads that emerge, the unequal arrangements that characterize much of the world leave large gaps between the real and the ideal. Again, I find myself in the midst of a contradiction.

I feel incredibly fortunate. Out of the infinite string of moments that is eternity, this path has emerged for me, connecting me to something greater than myself. It points me to something higher, revealing the potential for a better world close at hand. I can't say that I know for certain what that something is, but I know that we are all striving for it, working toward it, and we are doing so in conjunction with the entire universe around us.

The path is leading me to realize that, maybe, we can get closer to that something by lifting others up, instead of pushing others down to prop ourselves up. By lifting others up, we naturally rise higher as well. This path is solidifying that sense of responsibility I have felt growing inside of me. I can't explain injustice. I don't understand all of the suffering in the world. But, in the trails of compassion, cooperation, and harmony that emerge in its midst, perhaps I can find my place.

Emergent Trails

Align your eyes with mine.
Do you see what's past the veils?
Entwined, my soul with thine:
Do you feel what that entails?
Refined, our spirits shine,
To reveal it in a couplet:

Restoring self through paths divergent fails;
Together run through love's emergent trails.

So, here I am, sitting on this plane as the engines begin to vibrate, surrounded by others whose lives have brought them to this point. Despite all of my reflections, I find that doubts still linger. My mind is transported back to yesterday morning, as I slowly woke up and realized that, at least for two years, it would be the last time I would wake up in that bed, in that house, with my family close at hand. "What am I doing?" I asked myself. I finally started to understand just how big of a change this is all going to be, how much of a leap of faith it is. At that point, part of me felt helpless. As much as I hope that the next two years will be full of enjoyable and significant experiences, I just don't know what is going to happen. There are so many unknowns.

One thing I do know is that I will miss my family and friends. The past week has been full of time spent with the people who are so important in my life, and they will all be on my mind during my time overseas. Finally, I find myself coming to terms with the fact that this road is going to be difficult.

In this midst of this realization, other thoughts begin to flutter on the borders of my consciousness. Can I really know the motives at the very core of my being? Can I ever be completely sure that I am acting out of love and compassion, out of a pure desire to do right? I think I am, but is it possible that I am just trying to persuade someone, perhaps one of those friends or family members, of my own goodness? Is it all a show for someone else's benefit? How can I tell? How do I know? Maybe I can never know. Perhaps, the point is that I will never know all of the motivations that swim in the depths of my soul, but, regardless, I will continue to strive to do good.

Am I ready? Am I equipped, mentally, emotionally, spiritually, to be the best person I can be, to remain present, to appreciate the moment, to open my heart to a country and to the people in it, to give myself completely to this amazing opportunity?

The plane blasts forward. I am pressed against the back of my seat. The surface of the earth speeds past the window, and then drops away as we angle skyward. No turning back now.

The Waterfall of Grace

Reeling, wheeling, feeling, healing,
Twisting in the misting
Of a waterfall of grace;
Rumbling, tumbling, fumbling, humbling,
Praying as the spraying
Of the water hits my face.

Uncertainty of what you are,
While you can see my every scar,
How powerfully your droplets dart,
Pelt my skin, and flood my heart.

"Are you safe?" we asked of late.
Your silence served to incubate
The searching flames within the mind
Of each one who still feels so blind.

We are the thinkers, we are the dreamers,
We wonder what it means to be redeemers.
Then the water enters and reveals us,
And in the knowing of our flaws it heals us.

But standing empty in the squall,
I shudder. You're not safe at all.
With my healing comes a call
To plummet down the waterfall.

It's a risk, up on grace's cliff,
In the mist, finding your "what if?"
What if I allowed your love
To fill my heart, and then to shove?

My mind will never comprehend,
But in my heart it starts to blend.
Revealing is healing, and filling is willing
Me to become the love that is spilling,
Sowing, growing, showing, glowing,
Flowing, somehow knowing,
As I leap out into space.

As the plane begins to level out, my eyes catch a glimpse of the interface between land and sea far below. The eastern edge of the United States passes beneath us and starts to fade away. Looking further back, the sun is sinking toward the western horizon, and, as the horizon rises to meet it, a shifting kaleidoscope of colors is born, beginning in warm reds, oranges, and yellows, moving through faded blue-green pastels, and finishing with a deep violet as the darkened evening sky is pulled across the canvas above and around us. The first stars glint into view. The sun has set on the western hemisphere, and we are hastening to meet its rising in the east.

Fairly early in the flight, we are served dinner, and it starts me thinking about the pieces that make up our existence. Each day, our bodies take in new material and release old, expended material. The current cells in our bodies are constantly being replaced by new ones. The current molecules that make up those cells are being traded in and out all the time. If our bodies are constantly changing, taking in the new and dismissing the old, then who am I? What does it mean to be me, if I am always changing?

Similarly, our selves vary from moment to moment. In each subsequent, infinitesimal piece of time, our thoughts and experiences change. Over short timespans, these alterations might seem insignificant or even imperceptible, but they can build over the course of many moments. After a while, their aggregate effect can lead us to new ways of seeing and thinking. Eventually, I may look back at the person I used to be and discover my current self to be dramatically different.

So, we undergo continual change as the building blocks of matter and time move through us. In some ways, these changes can lead us to wonder where our uniqueness and individuality originate, what the concept of an enduring soul means in a universe of constant transformation and development. In other ways, they can give us a sense of the deep history in which we are involved. These individual atoms that pass through our bodies could, perhaps, be traced back to the beginning of everything, and so could this sequence of moments. We find ourselves directly linked to the entirety of the cosmic saga, from start to finish. Although only a small collection of atoms and hours makes up our individual, conscious, physical existence, the choices we make could have a profound impact on the future of those atoms and hours.

Do I have more influence than I realize? Perhaps I can bring about more change than I might think. Would I recognize myself if I saw myself truly living in the full potential of those universal connections of time and space, working to bring healing and peace in the midst of strife and pain? Will my time in Uganda teach me more about this possibility? How will I find myself changed, after taking the plunge and letting the tide take me?

On the Shores of the Sea

Yesterday I asked myself, "What would life have been,
If I had stayed with you on the shores of the sea,
Instead of walking out and wading in?"
If I never asked myself, "What's beyond the horizon?"
But as I watched the waves kissed by the morning breeze,
I resolved to chase the rising sun.

And so I let the tide take me,
Like going down a slide, faintly,
Sat back and let my mind break free,
To see the water with altered eyes.

Only standing on the sand to watch the surface flow,
Would have blinded me to the depths beneath,
Where the currents of our lives are known.

And so I let the tide take me,
Like going down a slide, faintly,
Sat back and let my mind break free,
To see the water with altered eyes

But it's always home I long for,
It's always you I sing for,
And always, ever more, each passing day.
So I hope you never think that
I never take time to think back
And imagine my return, though you might say,
The journey, it has changed me in many ways.

So one day, I'll float on back to the shores of the sea,
Bringing tales of truth, joy, and sorrowful tears,
And I wonder if you'll know it's me,

After I let the tide take me
Like going down a slide, faintly,
Sat back and let my mind break free,
To see the water with altered eyes,
And to know myself behind my disguise.

MOVEMENT 3 | TURNING

Storms of the Mind

Yellow and red, under deep violet blue,
Bending, descending, and changing in hue,
Darker and darker, 'til no more in view,
Blighting the bold and stark horizon.

Gathering clouds all collect in the night,
Covering over the strained dying light,
Darker and darker, 'til nary a sight
Shears through my field of steely reason.

Storms of the mind so conceal deeper fears,
Darker and darker, 'til rains hide the tears,
Often surprising, though, once tempest clears,
Fair are the stars when fell winds free them.

You, upon your yellow old rocking chair,
Sensitive always to my hidden care,
"Beautiful stars are," you said, "always there,
If you allow your soul to see them."

Expectations, assumptions, hardship, loneliness, frustration. As I begin to face the struggles associated with this experience, I find myself turning back toward my past, wondering if helpful grains of wisdom might have been left behind. Navigating through these storms can be difficult.

I've been away from the comfort and safety of training for fourteen days. Those initial ten weeks in the country, most of which were spent in Wakiso, a town close to Uganda's capital city of Kampala, are gradually beginning to fade. The members of my training group were distributed throughout that town, living with homestay families. I was with the Katambas, who lived at the edge of town on a farm with chickens, pigs, goats, and a cow or two. The first member of the family I had met was Robin, the mother, who spent her busy days cooking, cleaning, and digging.

In Luganda, the language spoken by the Buganda tribe in central Uganda, the word *okulima* – literally translated as "digging" – generally refers to agricultural work. A man named Frederick, whom I met on one of my first days in Wakiso, provided a possible explanation of this term. He said that farming is often something that people do out of necessity. With limited education and little chance for formal employment, people will start to farm in an effort to keep busy and to scratch out a living. Without much knowledge of farming methods, their labor begins by simply digging into the soil. Hopefully, over time, they and their children will learn and discover improved agricultural techniques, but Frederick's impression was that these farms still produce far less than their potential.

The father of my host family, Livingston, owned a small shop in town, where he sold a variety of basic items, like bread, rice, tea, and sugar. Every town in the country seems to contain dozens of these little, one-room shops that are near replicas of one another. A shop often opens shortly after sunrise and doesn't close until several hours after sunset, with one or two people managing it during that extended period of time. I saw less of Livingston, because he spent much of his time in town at the shop. The family had two older daughters, Martha and Faith, and a few younger kids were also running around all the time. In this environment, I quickly learned some of the basic tasks I would need to master, or at least perform with some level of success, to live in rural Uganda – bathing with a bucket of water, washing my clothes by hand, squatting in a pit latrine, and coming to terms with unpredictable and frequent power outages.

The trainees came together every morning at a training center on the other side of town, some of us hiking almost an hour along dirt roads, paved roads, and wooded paths. On rainy mornings, when my host mother would try to persuade me to stay at home, fearing I would fall sick, we braved the slippery, muddy paths, all but deserted in the rain. Upon reaching the training center, we launched into long days of language, cultural, and technical sessions, sometimes interesting, sometimes repetitive. Late in the afternoon, we embarked on the return journey back to our homestays, perhaps stopping in town to relax and spend time together outside of the intensive and occasionally stressful training environment.

As arduous as training could be, the group was helped along by a sense of mutual, shared experience. As tired as we might get, as out of place as we might feel from time to time, we had one another for support. This is not to say that the backing of the group was a panacea for all ills. For instance, as our stomachs slowly became acclimated to different varieties of bacteria and viruses, many of us still experienced quite a bit of discomfort.

During our first week in the country, before moving to Wakiso and beginning our homestays, we stayed together in a conference center called Banana Village. Married couples were given their own places, but the rest of us stayed together in large rooms, each with several bunk beds, separated by gender. We had about twice as many women in our group as men, so their rooms were much more crowded. Within a few days, a stomach virus was making its way through one of the women's rooms, putting several members of our group out of commission for at least twenty-four hours. It was not, for them, a pleasant introduction to the country.

I experienced my own episode of intestinal distress five weeks into training, while we were in Wakiso. One typical morning, I woke up feeling a bit off. I couldn't put my finger on anything specific, but I felt slightly queasy as I walked through town. I thought that if I could just reach the training center and sit down, I would feel better. I made it that far, but, as I sat through our morning language class, the nausea grew, I became light-headed, and I felt as if I were about to faint. I am not a stranger to this feeling. In grade school, I had a few fainting spells, usually right before lunch, when I was very hungry. This time, hunger was certainly not a factor. My host family was stuffing me to capacity at every meal. Fortunately, I didn't faint, and I was able to move to a bedroom in the training center, where Peace Corps medical staff left me to rest. Over the next two days, this room became the extent of my world. I slept, read, ate very little, and spent more time in the bathroom than I would care to admit. I felt horrible. I found some comfort in my thoughts, though, as they turned toward my mother, who, just a few years before, would have been the one caring for me in times of sickness.

One Note

Every night, I go to sleep, one chapter at an end,
And every morning, born anew, the next blank page to tend.
The story flowing through the pen springs from within and all around,
Each moment's thought a new creation, a chord of each life's sound.

Flipping through the pages of this ever-changing tale,
I notice ever-present notes, sustained, that never fail.
One of these, a mother's love, whose tone is rich and warm,
A gentle, rhythmic, beating heart, to calm the growing storm.

The note is heard, and also felt, deep within my soul,
An anchor, steady in the waves that pound the rocky shoal.
Though soft and sweet, I hear the note, knowing it will stay,
Even when I find myself half a world away.

Eventually, the sickness passed, and I returned to the training sessions and to my homestay family. And yet, this small interval of solitude had shown me something, something that I didn't completely grasp until training was over. In the middle of it, I had been given a few quiet days, during which I was almost completely alone with my thoughts. Up until that point, our training schedule had been so busy that I hadn't given myself time to consider some of the implications of this experience. Despite living with a Ugandan family for part of each day, I had been somewhat insulated inside of a cocoon filled with fellow trainees, and I didn't have a chance to appreciate the degree of separation between myself and the people across the ocean who are so special to me. Now, tonight, as I sit here alone in my house, two weeks after our training group graduated, became volunteers, and dispersed across the country to our individual sites, I am beginning to understand.

Today was one of the hardest days to get out of bed. The previous night, I dreamt that I was spending time with a very close friend. It was nothing breathtakingly exciting, but it was about someone I love very much. I usually don't remember dreams very well at all, but this one has lingered. Waking up with that sense of contentment and gladness, and then realizing that it was only a dream, that it was not real, made pulling myself out of bed very difficult. I wanted to fall back into the dream, and I found myself thinking about my friend all day.

Being so far away from the people who are important to me has been a challenge. Before leaving for Uganda, I had an idea of how hard it would be, but I didn't fully understand it until I experienced its reality. It was something I thought about on that initial plane ride, as the sun was rising on a part of the world that was new to me. In that moment, I was reminded that, even though this world can seem so vast, it is truly a small speck in the cosmos, and we are all quite close together. Maybe one afternoon, I had thought during that flight, I will gaze into the sky and glance at the sun, as someone I love across the sea wakes up to the light of that same star. In that moment, our eyes will be connected across thousands of miles, even if we are unaware. We are not as far apart as we might seem.

Is This You

The morning light is breaking,
Across a cloudless sky.
The birds begin their waking,
Singing as they flutter by,
And as the silence gently fades away,
I feel my heart start to heal,
For reasons I cannot explain.

Is this you? Is this you?
Were you here last night as the tears flowed down?
Is this how you help me through?

Somewhere in the world out there
Is a girl who I wish was here,
The kind of friend you'll always hold dear.
She's the one that I've been missing,

For what feels like a hundred years,
And as the earth revolves around the sun,
The universe begins to make things clear.

The mountain stream is flowing,
Trickling beneath the trees.
The birds watch the shadows knowing
That soon the stars above will gleam,
And as their music starts to fade away,
Twilight falls, but not for long,
And tomorrow they will sing just the same.

Is this you? Is this you?
Are you here tonight as the world goes round,
To show me what's really true?

Somewhere in the world out there,
She sees the same starry sky,
She sees the same sun start to rise.
The song of the birds is ringing,
And the same rule still applies.
Whether here or there or anywhere,
Our hearts are closer than geography implies.

All I have to do is think of you,
And the light returns to my eyes.

Even as I find myself missing these friends and family members, they act as a source of strength, especially in the increased solitude of the past several days. Despite the miles, my thoughts of them bring warmth and tenderness. My memories bring laughter and a smile. I am finding these reservoirs of joy, kindness, and patience to be important as I begin to navigate the new circumstances of my life.

As with anything, there are positives as well as difficulties. In my eyes, for instance, my living situation is quite comfortable, more so than I may have expected. During my senior year at Bucknell, when three other students and I were working on a water supply system for a village in Suriname, we were interacting with a Peace Corps Volunteer stationed in that village. When we visited, it was very much what I expected out of a "Peace Corps experience". This village was in the middle of a rainforest, and it could only be reached by boat. Electricity, running water, and paved roads were nowhere in sight. We slept in hanging hammocks or on mattresses on the floor, cocooned inside of white mosquito nets hanging just above our heads.

Now, in Uganda, I find myself living in Kalisizo, a very small and still relatively underdeveloped town, but a town nonetheless, just off of a paved, highly-trafficked road. Electricity is available, though often intermittent, and I sleep in a bed with a mosquito net draped above at a comfortable height. I am in a two-room house with plastered brick walls, a metal roof, and concrete floors, inside a compound with several other housing units. The entire compound has one outdoor water tap, fed by the town's piped supply, which operates a few times a week. In addition to a bedroom and a front room, where I have a few chairs, store the food I buy at the market, and cook using a propane stove, there is also a tiny room with a drain in the floor that leads outside. Here is where I bathe using a blue, twenty-liter bucket filled with water. Outside, the corner of the compound contains a set of three simple pit latrines, one of which is mine. It is different than my previous life, but this living situation feels relatively comfortable, and I feel that it will continue to be so for the next two years.

However, not everything is quite so comfortable. Take public transportation. I can already see that this part of my life is going to cause some anxiety and frustration over the next couple of years. Peace Corps Volunteers don't drive, perhaps rightly so, considering the poor condition of some roads and the extreme speeds employed by some drivers. As a result, public transportation is necessary when moving around the country. A number of options exist. On one end of the spectrum, large buses travel between Kampala (the capital city) and other major population centers throughout the country. The comfort level on these vehicles is decently high. Everyone sits in his or her own seat, and the seats are relatively large, although available leg room leaves a bit to be desired for a tall, bony Peace Corps Volunteer. The convenience of these buses is fairly low, however. Because they have many seats, they can take a long time to fill, meaning that I might still be sitting on a stationary bus a few hours after boarding. Once a bus does finally start to move, the stops it makes are fairly limited. Unless someone is traveling to a large city or town, another form of transportation may be needed to reach the desired destination.

Two varieties of minibuses are also available. One type, the coaster, is designed to carry twenty-eight passengers, and another type, the *matatu*, is meant to carry fourteen. These vehicles make more stops and travel to more places, and they often take less time to fill. However, the seats are smaller, and, sometimes, drivers will stuff more people inside than recommended. This makes for a much less comfortable ride, especially because the old seat padding is often quite thin and worn down. Whether or not a *matatu* or a coaster is overstuffed is generally dependent on location within the country and the presence or absence of police checkpoints along the route.

Once a traveler gets close to his or her final destination, a few more options present themselves. Motorcycle taxis, called *boda-bodas*, will carry anywhere from one to four passengers (plus luggage). These motorcycles will go anywhere, but they are more expensive than other possibilities. Also, because they are seen as the most dangerous options on the road, often snaking in and out of traffic with abandon, Peace Corps Volunteers are not allowed to use them. The other alternative is a four-door sedan, almost always an old Toyota Corolla or a similar model. Personal space is far from sacred in these vehicles. It is common to fit at least ten people in one of these cars – six layered in the backseat, two in the front passenger's seat, and one in the driver's seat, plus the driver.

Masaka is a large town about thirty kilometers north of Kalisizo, with a number of amenities that Kalisizo is lacking. I can see myself traveling to and from Masaka relatively frequently in the months to come. These small cars, where I am packed in with nine other souls, are the most common form of transportation available: rarely comfortable, often frustrating, always an adventure.

The Ride Home

Sitting at the taxi spot,
As the sun descends the sky,
Is a car with space that's not a lot,
So you'd better not be shy.
Climb into a cramped backseat

And greet the seven strangers.
Together you'll face the stifling heat
And assorted roadway dangers.

But it's not yet quite time to go,
For first, you must wait.
Two more souls can fit, you know.
Who cares if you get there late?
Now that all the space is taken,
You embark upon the road,
Any leg room now forsaken,
Along with the traffic code.

Watch the trees fly past the window
That can't move up or down.
With every bounce, the roof seems too low,
But then you see your town.
Relief flows through your veins to your toes,
Before your blood returns there.
Despite the dust filling up your nose,
Breathe deep, you've made it somewhere...

Coming into Uganda, I had no idea what to expect regarding public transportation. Truthfully, at the beginning, I knew nothing about where I would be living or what I would be doing. As much as I tried to come in with no expectations or assumptions about what would happen, I suppose it was inevitable that I would still have a few, based mostly on my previous trips to Nicaragua and Suriname. I think, in the back of my mind, I expected to be stationed in a more remote, rural area. While Kalisizo is surrounded by fairly secluded, rural villages, the town itself contains about 10,000 people, several primary schools, some places of worship, and a few secondary schools. It also sits on a major road, which connects Kampala to the Tanzanian border. In addition to the cars and *matatus* that run along this road, quite a few trucks are seen as well, transporting commercial goods between the two countries.

I also did not expect to be spending much of my time working in an office. I had always thought that the typical Peace Corps experience involved living and working in a rural village community with no offices, no electricity, and no computers. And yet, over the past two weeks, the majority of my time has been spent in an office. In Uganda, most Peace Corps Volunteers are either placed at schools or with non-governmental organizations (NGOs), which have specific missions and projects within local communities. About half of the volunteers in the country are in the education sector, and they are placed at primary schools, secondary schools, and primary teachers' colleges, where aspiring teachers are educated. The remaining volunteers are either in the economic development sector or the health sector, and these usually end up working with NGOs. As a water, sanitation, and hygiene volunteer, I fall within the health sector, and I was placed with an organization called Brick by Brick Uganda, which has an office in Kalisizo. To be fair, the term "office" might be a bit of a stretch. It consists of two small, dark rooms with metal, padlocked doors. Inside, we have some chairs and desks where we can put our laptops and plug them in when the electricity is on. The off-white, plastered brick walls are made slightly more interesting by the maps and photographs hanging from nails hammered into the plaster.

Brick by Brick Uganda is a small NGO that partners with primary schools in Rakai District, the area where Kalisizo is located. Much of its work concerns infrastructure – renovating classrooms, installing water tanks, building libraries. Earlier this year, with the help of another Peace Corps Volunteer who recently completed his service, the organization founded a construction company that employs local masons and focuses on using and promoting Interlocking Stabilized Soil Bricks (ISSBs). ISSBs are reported to be more environmentally friendly than locally-produced burned bricks, and they can be used to build a variety of structures, including classrooms, latrines, and water tanks. I am still early in the process of finding my place in this organization. So far, besides a few visits to our partner schools and construction sites, I have spent most of my time in the office interacting with Max, Brick by Brick's program coordinator.

Most of our work together has focused on improving the company's marketing efforts – designing informational brochures, creating business cards for Max, setting up meetings with potential clients. This is an area I have no experience with, and I was certainly not expecting to be engaged in business marketing during my Peace Corps service. I was also not expecting certain attitudes from some of the people around me. I am beginning to understand that a number of people have assumptions about someone from the United States, and it can be difficult to navigate those assumptions.

I don't think this is true of my coworkers at Brick by Brick, but at least some people in Kalisizo seem to expect me to act a certain way, to have access to a certain quantity of money and resources, or to be able to do certain things for them. I don't know if anything could have completely prepared me for the unrealistic notions of some of the people around me. Then again, I am beginning to realize that my own ideas about this experience may have been overly idealistic as well, that everything would be pure and perfect, an unbroken path on which I would save the world, at least a little bit. Sometimes, as I try to traverse this uneven landscape, I get the feeling that I've been dropped in the middle of a tangled net of expectations, assumptions, and very real issues. It can be very complicated and confusing.

A few nights ago, when the power was out and I was surrounded by darkness, I was thinking about these difficulties. For some reason, my mind recalled a visit to my grandfather's farm the day before I began this journey. I remember sitting across the kitchen table from him, my father's father, having a very slow and deliberate conversation, a conversation between two people often content to keep speech to a minimum. The topics ranged from the time I would be leaving the next day to a comparison of the behavior of cows and pigs. I remember looking around the farmhouse and suddenly realizing that time had seemed to slow down in this place. I realized that it was all right to simply sit and be.

Instead of worrying about what might happen the next day, we took time to enjoy the flowers along the path as we walked back to my car. We examined the tomato vines growing next to the porch, we watched the butterflies hovering over the plants to the left of the path, and Grandpa mentioned that it might be time to trim the hedge on the right. After giving him a hug, getting in the car, and waving one last time as I turned out of the driveway, time slowly returned to normal, but the feeling that had developed in my heart, a feeling born from the unspoken wisdom of a much more experienced man, remained.

In the blackness of the Kalisizo night, as a single candle flickered in my window, my thoughts turned toward my other grandfather, my mother's father, whom my brother and I affectionately call Pop-Pop.

He passed away several years ago, while I was still in high school. He had decades of construction experience, which I could certainly use now. I found myself wondering what he would think of this experience. I found myself wondering what unspoken wisdom he would impart.

Unspoken Wisdom

Somewhere in the darkened silence trembled
A single, subtle thought,
Someplace there my centered focus stumbled
On silhouettes of naught.
Some familiar one that thought resembled,
A strange idea fraught
Somehow with the sounds my soul has mumbled
When angels have been sought.
Somewhere in the dark your thought assembled
From other realms here brought,
Something left my comprehension humbled
While inner logic fought.
"Are you truly here tonight?" I trembled
And wondered what you sought.
Somehow then unspoken wisdom tumbled
Into my jumbled thought,
And suddenly,
My walls of worry crumbled,
Revealing what I ought
To do, to see, to truly be:
The one your wisdom taught.

These doubts, these difficulties, these thoughts that have compelled me to turn back toward the memories of life before this journey, perhaps they suggest that this experience is more complex, more ambiguous, and less straightforward than I had previously imagined. The world that I had longed to save is bigger than what I have made it out to be, than what my limited perspective has seen. Do I even know what "saving the world" means? Can that enigmatic goal, even on a much smaller level, be reasonable for me? How much is out there that is beyond me, so far out in the unknown that I cannot even fathom its possibility?

At the same time, while I may find myself feeling like a small speck on the surface of a planet that has just grown much bigger, I am not alone. I am never alone.

Perhaps, I need to take a step back, be still and present in the moment, and listen to the world that is around me. I am beginning to realize that my time in Uganda is about more than helping those I see as being less fortunate. It's about truth. It's about finding a window into a greater reality, revealing new ideas, as well as misconceptions I hold about myself and the world around me. I do not yet know what is in these droplets of truth. I need to let myself be taken into this experience, to turn toward it and open my eyes, my mind, my heart. There is truth here, in the good and the bad, in the intersection between the real and the ideal. In living it, and in working to find a lasting peace that allows me to encounter it with compassion and love, perhaps I can shine a light and begin to illuminate it.

Here and There

Likened to when spent atoms of skin
Descend to the ground as I climb,
Specks of the soul flake off as I flow
Through time and through spaces sublime,
Imprinting themselves upon where the heart delves.
They stymie my trite, easy rhyme.

Can ever I describe, with phrases not clichéd and worn,
The mixing bowl, rough-hewn and jagged
That tempers me each morn?
Night's starlit, silent calm, pure-rendered and imbued with peace,
Reacting, sometimes nigh-explosive,
With sunlit, true-lived grease,
Clashing one moment, then woven together the next,
Mind and reality, always unfrozen,
Learning, relating, reflexed,
Eternally circling, peeling, revealing
Truth nested under life's text.

Specks of the soul flake off as I flow
And link me to points where I've been,
Shining unseen, like stars in a dream,
Mining still deeper within,
Here and there finding small droplets of diamonds,
Balanced upon the edge of a knife,
You and I trying to stay their declining
Until their primed truths burst forth into life.

MOVEMENT 4 | FINDING

A Day at the Office

In a chair behind a wooden desk,
In an office all alone,
I sit, all quiet, a thoughtful diet,
To contemplate how time has flown,
To prepare, all stern and statuesque,
To learn from what I've known.
But wait, what's this? I reminisce,
And recognize the sudden tone.

Small shapes approach the open door
And step in from the light,
As if on cue, sing "How are you?"
And grin, their eyes now twinkling bright.
Some stand, some sit upon the floor,
And grab the pens I've placed in sight.
The troupe of kids removes the lids,
And so proceeds to write.

A few view posters on the wall
And copy what they see.
A word, a phrase, will catch their gaze,
And, proud, they'll bring their work to me.

For others, letters lose their thrall,
And flowing pens foam free,
Creating halls and waterfalls
That propagate themselves with glee.

And often, they might misbehave.
I frequently may be annoyed,
But in the mess and recklessness,
These interruptions cross a void.
In this safe space, they learn, embrace
Creative traits that they've employed,
And I remember, life's renewing ember
Comes unexpectedly to be enjoyed.

I came into the office late this morning expecting to do some work. Over the past several months, we have been busy, as our team of masons has been trained to build more structures, as more potential clients have been contacting us, and as the company has begun turning a modest profit. In the midst of it all, I have found myself focusing less on marketing and business development, and more on project planning, construction cost estimates, and some engineering design. I am certainly grateful for this shift. Even though I still do not have much experience with construction management or with structural design, it is more closely related to the environmental engineering education I was equipped with when I arrived in Uganda.

A significant factor that has enabled this shift in my role is the fact that another Peace Corps Volunteer started working with Brick by Brick about eight months ago. Griffin was in my training group, but she was placed in a nearby town with an organization that was not a good fit. This organization seemed to expect her to bring money and resources when she arrived, but that is not how the Peace Corps operates. Unfortunately, I have heard stories from a number of volunteers, revealing that these unrealistic expectations are not so uncommon, perhaps because, historically, foreigners supported by international non-profits have often come into local areas wielding substantial funds and resources. In any case, the situation was not a good one for Griffin, and, after a few months, she was able to move to Kalisizo and begin working with Brick by Brick instead. I am happy to say that Brick by Brick has a better understanding of the

Peace Corps model, and I feel fortunate in my own site placement.

Griffin has a background in economics, making her much better suited to those business development concerns that had initially vexed me, thereby allowing me to focus on topics more related to my own field. Even so, over the course of a week, our technical work was easily sidetracked, as we often needed to help one of our coworkers write an email, create a spreadsheet, or proofread a report. It can be enlightening to realize how many seemingly minor tasks we take for granted as people who grew up using computers or using English as the primary language spoken by our families and friends. For others who lack this experience accumulated over many years, performing one of these supposedly small assignments can become a difficult, time-consuming, and painstaking ordeal. As we endeavor to ensure that Brick by Brick's work can be maintained after our service is complete, we understand that these tasks are important building blocks for much of what the organization does and hopes to do in the future. So, these concerns, as tedious as they can be for all of us, often take priority.

As a result, I will sometimes find myself coming into the office on a weekend, when I can work in solitude on my own tasks. That was my intention today, a Sunday. Now that the company has begun accumulating a small profit, we are starting to use that money to fund the infrastructure work we do in local primary schools. The long-term goal of the construction company is that it will be a significant, alternative source of funds for the projects that have always been supported by donations coming from the United States. The company could provide a local and more sustainable source of finances for projects that create a better educational environment for students, hopefully giving them a greater chance to break out of the cycles of disease, poverty, and unemployment that plague the families served by these poorly-funded public schools.

As the current year comes to a close, our plan is to use the company's profits to build a cost-effective and environmentally-conscious kitchen facility at one of our partner schools. I have been working on designing and costing the kitchen structure, and I have also been researching something called a rocket stove, which is more efficient than the cooking system used in most homes and schools. Usually, when cooking large quantities of food, a three-stone fire is used, which consists simply of three stones or blocks, arranged in a horizontal triangle, with a wood fire in the middle. The cooking pot sits on the stones and is heated by the fire underneath. This method is extremely inefficient and requires quite a bit of firewood. The quantities of wood needed can be quite expensive for a school. At the same time, deforestation has become a significant problem in Uganda, and the largest contributing factor is the use of firewood for cooking. On top of that, these fires often generate a great deal of smoke, creating air quality concerns that can harm the health of the people doing the cooking. The rocket stove is designed to heat the cooking pot much more efficiently, so that less firewood is needed and less smoke is generated. In the long run, it can be cheaper, healthier, and better for the environment.

Today, I had wanted to make some progress with this project, but, as often happens when I find myself alone in the office, young kids who live nearby started to wander in. When I'm not alone, my coworkers will make them go away, but I am a bit of a pushover. Inevitably, I find myself distracted, and they do, on occasion, get too loud and boisterous, which may lead me to finally usher them out. For the most part, though, once the initial annoyance of the disruption wears off, I find that I enjoy their presence, perhaps because they have grown accustomed to me as well. I give some of them coloring books to use, while others will sit beside me or on my lap, watching what I am doing. These kids do not have much, but they are not the caricatures of starving, diseased, dejected children we in the United States sometimes see on television. They play, they enjoy life, they have friends, and I seem to have become one of those friends. I may not go home today with all of my work done, but I might find myself feeling renewed and a bit more connected to this place that has become my home.

The Walk Home

Sunbeams, skirting westward treetops, glance across the open door,
Eyelids heavy, fingers weary, signaling the close of day,
Ready now to start the journey, traveled many times before,
Through the varied scenes and settings on the well-worn way.

Looking down, a slender shadow, shaped by setting sun behind,
Looking up, the shifting pillows, swollen clouds that slowly dance,

Looking straight ahead I notice woven threads of life, entwined
With the land and one another, all this in a glance.

Laundry strung across the alley, pigs and chickens sit below,
While their keepers cook (since morning), wood and charcoal fires glow,
Little ones from school are coming, past the vendors on the road
Selling roasted, meaty morsels or a bike's fruit load.

Walking on the stony streets, with rows of shops not quite the same,
Walking on the dusty paths, beside a pickup football game,
Walking on the sloping soil, just before my simple home,
In a compound filled with neighbors, here I cease to roam.

Through the varied scenes and settings, now I stop and, settled, stay,
Knowing life will go on rolling. "Let it come," I say.

As I leave the office and begin to make my way to my house on the
other side of town, I realize that the walk itself has become
something of a meditative experience, revealing the life around me
and the home that I have found here. The birds flying overhead, the
livestock getting out of the way, the people going about their
business, they all begin to open me to the diversity and newness of
each moment, the opportunity to learn, if I can just allow it to come
and dwell within me.

My experience has certainly not become an unending parade of
pleasant and illuminating events. Sometimes, as I'm walking the
streets of Kalisizo, I feel like the pale color of my skin is the only
thing others see as they look at me. But other times, when I stop and
am able to have a conversation with someone, I feel a connection
that goes far beyond anything related to external appearance. We care
about the same things, we want our friends to be safe and happy, we
want children to have good teachers, and we want to learn from each
other. Just in the space of a few minutes, or even a few seconds, each
of us can move beyond seeing the other person as someone who is
foreign, strange, and unfamiliar, and we can start to see an individual
who is cut from the same cloth.

Yesterday, I walked past a woman. "*Mzungu, mpa ssente*," she said:
"Foreigner, give me money." The word *mzungu* is usually not used in
a deliberately hostile or degrading way, but its repetition over time

can certainly begin to weigh on one's soul, accentuating differences and provoking a feeling of being out of place. I told her, as politely as I could, that I was not able to give money: "*Nyabbo, sisobola okuwa ssente.*" She walked away. As is usually the case when this happens, I also started to walk away, frustrated with the fact that we live in a world where this happens quite a lot, wondering what the answer is, what the best response is. But then, another woman came up to me and started speaking to me in English. Her name was Lydia, and she showed me where she lives, introduced me to two of her kids, Lydia and Rachel, and told me that her son Earnest, who is away at school, has hair similar to my long, wavy locks. I expressed some disbelief at that, as I have not seen a Ugandan man with hair longer than a half an inch, except for a few self-proclaimed Rastafarians in Kampala. Lydia also showed me her cow, which needed to have its horns sanded off at the top because they were so big. It was a very simple conversation, but I found it to be restorative. By the end of it, she even had her kids calling me "Uncle John".

I don't know if she had seen my exchange with the first woman and wanted to lift my spirits or had randomly decided to start talking to me, but it did help me to feel a little better. And it kept me from falling into the trap, from starting to make the generalization that every Ugandan sees me and immediately thinks that I might be a source of money. Lydia's greeting helped to show me that I am valued, just for being a human being.

We can't just see people in one dimension. Especially when viewing the world through a wide lens, we are bombarded with statistics, and we inevitably lump people into categories – impoverished and rich, sick and healthy, malnourished and well-fed. While these categories certainly represent difficult and painful parts of the lives of some, the words do not define their entire lives. Every single person has hopes and dreams, likes and dislikes, virtues and faults, just like I do. Their dignity and inherent value as unique individuals are of prime importance, regardless of their perceived place in society.

Take the case of one extremely broad category of people – women. In many parts of the world, women have faced, and continue to face, hardships and prejudices not experienced by their male counterparts. While progress is being made at various levels in Uganda, the country is certainly no exception to these issues. So often, I hear about and see female Peace Corps Volunteers who must face various forms of sexism, discrimination, and harassment every day. Ugandan women encounter these difficult conditions throughout their lives. Despite this, many also lead impressive lives. They always seem to be busy, cooking, cleaning, taking care of children, collecting firewood, fetching water, farming, running shops. And yet, their incredible work ethic and unfathomable contributions frequently go unrecognized.

It can become easy for me to feel sorry for this broad group of people, but if being sorry is the sole limit of my understanding and interaction with them, I am missing so much that is important. Simply seeing them as victims strips them of their dignity as unique, creative, multidimensional individuals.

Some of these amazing women live in my compound, always busy, but also always full of life and joy. Sarah, who cooks and cleans for my landlady's family, and who occasionally does my laundry for me, has been especially kind to me. Over the past several weeks, on certain evenings before the sun has completely left the sky, Sarah has knocked on my door and invited me outside to eat jackfruit with her and some of the other ladies and children in the compound.

Jackfruit, or *ffene*, is a very large fruit with rough, hard, green skin. Inside are sweet, yellow seedpods. Because this fruit is so big, one person will usually hack into it with a machete, split it into sections, and then share it with a group of people. This is what happens in our compound. While I'm sitting there, I feel like I am becoming more a part of this tiny community. These women have let me in, and, together, we learn more about the true realities of our lives, the difficulties as well as the delights. We are all just people, relaxing, laughing, and eating fruit.

Under the Shade of a Jackfruit Tree

Sitting
In a plastic chair
Under the shade of a jackfruit tree,
Neighbors come to share,
Splitting,
Somewhat evenly,
Sections of fruit, and the children smile

As they dance with glee,
Spitting
Seeds into a pile.
Bathed in their kindness, I find I've been,
Somehow all the while,
Fitting in.

From the beginning of training, Peace Corps stressed how important it is for volunteers to integrate themselves into the local community. What exactly does this mean?

I thought I knew. I thought, from my previous international experiences, that I understood, but living in a place for an extended period of time is very different from visiting a place for a few weeks. The service trips I had participated in before coming to Uganda each lasted between seven and ten days. I learned quite a bit in that span of time, but I certainly didn't get the full picture, complete with complexity and ambiguity. Going to Nicaragua for a week, for instance, I thought that I was living and working in solidarity with the Nicaraguan people. All the while, I was insulated from those people and their country by the group I was with, our guides and translators, and a guarded, fenced-in compound. In Suriname, we found ourselves much closer to the true lives of those around us, but our group still had one another, our guide and translator, and the knowledge that, whatever happened, we would be flying out of the country in a few days.

Living in Uganda, more or less on my own, is different. Certainly, some things still set me apart from those around me. I cook with a propane stove, rather than charcoal or wood. I have a laptop computer. I take malaria prophylaxis every week. On the other hand, life here is not some surreal experience in what seems to be another world, which may be what I had unconsciously expected. For one thing, I am not living in a little hut in the middle of a jungle, surrounded by people who have never had contact with the outside world. Most houses in Kalisizo have brick walls and metal roofs, many people have television sets, and some of the more affluent residents own cars. More importantly, though, those around me are regular people, living their lives. Life here is simply that – life.

And that's how I have come to feel about my own existence in this place. I am just someone living his life. I wake up and walk through town to our office, greeting some kids along the way. I occasionally turn the office into a daycare center for neighboring little ones when none of my coworkers are around. I stop at the market on my way home. I cook dinner and then read or watch a television show on my computer to relax before going to bed. What's so incredible, so surreal, so out of the ordinary, about that?

As I live my life, I am coming to realize that I have, perhaps unwittingly, become more integrated into this community. I think it has occurred less as a result of my own efforts and more from the openness of those around me. Admittedly, despite my training, I am still something of a novice with Luganda, probably because we usually work in English at the office, and because most people in town know at least some English and want to practice it when talking to me. Admittedly, it is pretty easy for me to get lost in my work, to spend all day at the office – like I did today – and then come home, either to do a little more work or just to sit in solitude and relax.

However, even though I don't understand everything that is said to me, even though I don't always open myself up to the wealth of experiences around me, the people here want to include me in their lives. It's been fun. Just in the past month or so, I went to a graduation party for my landlady's daughter, I visited two of Max's kids at their boarding schools, and I've spent more than a few evenings sitting with women and children in my compound, talking and eating jackfruit or sugarcane. I don't really like chewing on sugarcane. I feel like the only thing it's doing for me is destroying my teeth, but I also don't want to say no when I'm invited. One woman even cooked lunch for me last Saturday. I didn't ask her to do that, and I didn't even know she was doing it until she knocked on my door to give me two plates of food. She just did it, out of neighborliness and the goodness of her heart.

These simple acts of kindness and acceptance have done more to bring me into the community than anything I could have done on my own. As a result, this place has become something familiar, a world that is not so different from what I knew before. It is somewhere I can learn, work, and live. I am so fortunate to have this opportunity, to cross a divide that is actually imaginary.

I sometimes cannot believe that I've already spent more than a year in this country. Some of my memories from before this time, memories from those last few weeks in the United States, still seem very fresh in my mind. Other times, though, I feel like I have been living here for much longer. Walking back to my house after a day's work, I recognize neighbors and feel as if I am in the right place. Every time I return to Kalisizo after a few days away, I pass kids who know me and want to practice the only English phrases they've learned.

"Johnny, how are you?"

"I am fine," I call back, and it's true. I feel as if I am coming home.

After a day at the office, the walk home, and an evening eating jackfruit with my neighbors, I lie in my bed, which, after a year of use, has a permanent dip that fits my body. I drift off to sleep, contented and comfortable.

On a Lazy, Rainy Morning

Fade into the gentle tapping,
Surface from a silent dream,
Eyes and ears sedately open,
Catch the cloudy, dripping theme,
Feel at once the mind relaxing,
Wash the soul, restored and clean,
Cool serenity adorning,
On a lazy, rainy morning.

Venture through the flowing sheeting
Covering the streets around,
Few appear to trade a greeting,
Yet the stoic cows are found,
Still, perhaps refreshed, and silent,
For a time the heat is drowned,
Airborne rivers calm its burning,
Life can pause to watch the morning.

Something in that steady sound
Streaming down each soiled mound,
Smoothing out uneven ground,
Fills the heart and quells its storming,
On a lazy, rainy morning.

I awake to a cool, steady rain. This variety of precipitation is fairly common here during the wet season, and it can be incredibly relaxing. The cool temperature, the gentle, steady tapping of raindrops on the roof, and the general lack of activity outside all help to keep me in bed longer than normal.

Everything seems to happen more slowly when it rains. People stay inside, if they can, and some may not go to work. Shops open later or don't open at all. Goats and chickens find spots on porches and verandas where they have some shelter. I sleep in, take my time getting ready once I do pull myself out of bed, and then take a leisurely walk to the office in my rain jacket. With very few people outside, I put most of my focus on the tiny streams and rivulets that only exist during and immediately after these periods of precipitation. They snake along the sides of roads and through uneven paths, here stalling and pooling, there racing and falling. The water does something to my soul. It slows things down, quiets my thoughts to a gentle murmur, and stretches my vision to see the connections of life that flourish through the running of the water.

Then there are the cows. While people and most animals try to find some shelter and stay there, the cows stand, still and silent, in the middle of the field, as the water washes across their backs. Maybe the rain cools their skin, usually hot under the gaze of the sun. Maybe they see something deeper in the rain, something penetrating through the heavy air, giving relief amid trouble and pain. Maybe I have seen it, too, in the gentle ripples of the streams, in the light that passes through each raindrop as it briefly gleams, in the eyes of those who know this life is more than what it seems.

Penetrating Grace

I mostly act an introvert,
An introspective stoic,
While, inwardly, I long for love,
But you, you must see through it.
Why else would you love me so
When shown my guarded face?
Unless the gift be freely given
Through penetrating grace.

There is a message here, strung together in these experiences that have touched me. There is a deep-seated idea with great significance for our lives. The person and the relationship, the connection to that person, these are paramount, more so than anything else, more so than the message itself. To me, this is the grace that can penetrate our lives. This is the mercy, the compassion, the kindness that can transcend boundaries and borders. These people, in this place, have been showing me, and perhaps I am starting to see. Through their openness, their acceptance, their example, I am beginning to find my own ability and willingness to connect deeply and to love.

It is not simplistic charity. It is not merely an opportunity to do good. It is not an endorsement of any specific paradigm of foreign aid or development work. These are abstracts, concepts, ideas, which may fall to pieces in the face of reality, of truly lived circumstances. No idea is universal enough to apply perfectly in every conceivable situation. If we put our faith in these intangible notions, our faith may disappoint, and it may shatter, leading to cynicism and despair. I know. I have felt myself beginning to go in that direction from time to time. That path is easy and nearly frictionless.

But I have been shown a better way, one that does not focus on easy fixes and quick solutions. It is a harder road – a longer road – that dwells on the relationship and sees each soul as precious, essential, and full of dignity.

It is, perhaps, relatively simple and plain in theory. "Love others." Truly putting it into practice, however, can be much more difficult, for we cannot fully love someone unless we know and have some understanding of that person's life. How did I see Africa before coming to Uganda? Was my impression similar to that of many others in the United States? Did I see it in only one dimension, as a place filled with poverty, disease, conflict, and pain – as a suffering, starving, dying continent in need of help? No doubt, scars and hard realities are present, but they do not complete the story. They do not give us a full portrait of life. There is so much more. There is so much that is good. I see life, I feel warmth, and I encounter beauty.

Regardless of my previous, naïve ideas about this place, I cannot now simply see the Ugandan people as poor. Think of their families, their children, their communities. They are not poor. They have a different kind of wealth, and many lead fulfilling lives. These souls are not a part of this world simply to be saved, to give some of us an opportunity to exercise a spirit of compassion, to give us a target where we can focus our charity. An idea can never become more important than a person, and these are real people, living in a real place. There is more here than suffering. I know that now, because they have shown me. It is in living together, in our relationships and connections, that we move forward.

The Great Idea

In crystal palaces high on a hill
I used to spend my days,
Dreaming in sparkling rooms ever still,
Stuck in an abstract maze.

Seeking to solve life's lingering queries
Atop my cold, quartz chair,
Great ideas and glittering theories
Swept down the glassy stair.
They left by way of an emerald arch
So smooth and finely pearled,
And issued forth in a near-endless march
Upon the rugged world.

But why, oh why, did they not bring us nigh
To light yet thinly veiled?
Some, though embraced, soon doomed many to die.
Others fizzled and failed.

And then, I saw her standing there,
Pain in her eyes, a heart full of care,
Waiting for me to break out,
To crack this secluded, sterile lair
And hear life's raw, whispered shout.

We felt the earth in all her prime,
Touched by her cries, through the dust and the grime,
We loved what we were to find:
People surviving, sharing their time,
As theories shrunk in my mind.

Ideas do play a purpose, but fall
To love's tiniest plea.
The great idea, which stands above all,
Is you, is she, is we.

MOVEMENT 5 | SPEAKING

Fantasy and Fairy Tale

It has been said upon the high street,
Where saviors tread on whitewashed concrete,
That the people down below need our help to grow,
We their roads must pave, so them we can save,
But upon this trail,
The statements sound so stale.
In the end, they're nothing more than
Fantasy and fairy tale.

We have been fed a simple story
In which we've read of aid and glory
For the ones who sacrifice, feeding helpless mice,
But from here we see our equality.
Truthful winds prevail,
The pages prove so frail.
In the end, they're nothing more than
Fantasy and fairy tale.

Some see faceless outlines from afar,
Never knowing who they are,
But their light shines in the dark,
Ever showing their own spark.
Draw us near to faces clear,
Drain our fear of the stranger here.

I think, instead of storied disguise,
We might be led to use our own eyes
To see those who far surpass what the legends cast,
Often called the least, beggars at the feast.
Pull away the veil,
And walk the strangers' trail.
If you meet them, you'll find more than
Fantasy and fairy tale.

Sometimes, I skip lunch. My three coworkers, Max, Prossy, and Suzan, usually eat at a restaurant in town, and I often go with them. The restaurant's menu consists of a variety of starchy staples and protein sauces. Patrons choose one sauce – I usually order peas or beans – and some assortment of starches. My starch plate commonly contains rice, *posho* (made from maize flour), and *matooke* (a local staple made from mashed green bananas). Because large pots filled with each option have been cooking in the back for hours, we are served within about two minutes of ordering, and we receive a lot of food – a full plate of starch and a full dish of sauce. After eating like this for a few days in a row, I need a break. So, sometimes, I skip lunch.

Yesterday, I skipped lunch and, as a result, found myself alone in the office. This time, instead of young kids running past the door and eventually entering, a man who was in town doing missionary work happened to pass by. Upon seeing me, he made his way into the office, and we talked for a few minutes about the work each of us was doing. At the end of this amiable discussion, as he was turning to leave, he said, "Thank you for the sacrifice." Taken by surprise and unsure how to respond, I mumbled some incoherent acknowledgment as he walked out the door. Perhaps, before coming here, I considered Peace Corps service to be a sacrificial endeavor. But, in view of what I have learned over the past months, do I still see it in this light?

There are still times when I feel a sense of loss as I realize that, by being here, I am missing family, friends, and important events in their lives. But is this so uncommon? If sacrifice is defined in this way, almost anything anyone does is likely to have some small element of sacrifice to it. Any decision might involve sacrificing a job opportunity, regular contact with certain people, or comfortable modes of transportation. In this regard, my experience does not seem so dissimilar from anyone else's in the grand scheme of things. And, along with the costs of my decisions, I have also gained benefits and new perspectives, some that have corrected illusions and fantasies about others and about myself.

Some of these new perspectives have uncovered imperfections within myself that I might rather have left alone. Have I, then, sacrificed a sheltered conception of who I am? At the beginning of my time here, while I certainly did not state it explicitly, I might have subconsciously believed myself to be a good and special person for doing this thing, and I saw myself as a calm and collected figure able to handle adversity with grace and ease. I had a certain degree of idealism and sentimentality about me.

Over time, as my idealism has been tempered by the raw experience of reality not living up to my hopes, a certain amount of skepticism has crept into my thoughts. I question more than before, and I doubt my own goodness more than before. I know that I am not an individual with an extraordinary reserve of patience and calm. I have discovered a significant temper that flares up once in a while, as the frustrations and realities of this experience knock me down over and over again.

The past several months have brought my personality and my unadorned soul out into the light, allowing me to see the scratches, the bruises, and the dents. It's hard, within the moment (or when looking back on a moment), to realize that it is not one of my best. It's hard to discover how this world can threaten to make me more jaded, more pessimistic, more devoid of compassion, how it can tear down my abstractions and ideals about how things should be. It's hard to find myself, and to be not quite satisfied with what I find.

But is this really a sacrifice? In the end, I'm glad to realize that these parts of me exist. Perhaps it's important to be not quite satisfied, because it pushes me toward a path of growth and learning. It's important to understand that I could be nudged down a road that leads to pessimism or despair. I occasionally see myself turning in that direction. On the whole, I love what I'm doing, but that can be easy to forget when the frustrations build. It can be easy for me to become hard, closed, and unfriendly. But witnessing those parts of myself is a step toward overcoming them, with the help of those around me. By closing myself off in an attempt to exclude frustrations, I am also shutting out positive influences.

No, this is not a sacrifice. I have the opportunity to do something I love. Doing it means that I also miss other things, but they will reappear again. Though joy and love often mingle with disappointment and difficulty, perhaps this process can make the positive stronger. Though I have come to see many of my faults and blemishes more clearly, perhaps, in the end, that knowledge can make me a better person.

Who Am I

Who am I to speak of you as if I understand your life?
Who am I to tell your shaded tale of nuanced happiness and strife?
Who am I to comprehend your unique point of view?
Can I feel the sharp-edged knife slicing roughly through?
Can I know the ache of biting hunger
Or the bitter taste of stubborn thirst?
Can I see your hopes, now rent asunder,
Cut out from this play ne'er once rehearsed?
Could I hear the joy, when you were younger,
Ringing then before you knew the word
That dampens now your soul, like halted thunder?
"Injustice!" Can I feel what you've endured?

Who am I to speak of you as if I've walked your broken trail?
But, who am I to brush aside the life, which hides, for me, behind a veil?
We'll ensure your still, small voice can penetrate the slough,
So that all can hear your tale, filled with truth of you.

Do these personal realizations, though, give me any authority to comment on the circumstances here or to suggest possible paths forward? With my heightened sense of self, have I also gained a reliable sense of life in this place?

I like to talk about how we are all so similar, how very little separates me from a Ugandan, but certain things do distinguish us. I can't simply refuse to acknowledge that. Although there is undoubtedly a common humanity among all people, I am also aware of differences that result from our distinct cultural lenses and the specific conditions each individual has faced. Even after living in

Uganda for more than a year, I still can't say that I know the experience of a "typical Ugandan". Yes, I have seen things, I have heard stories, I have worked with many Ugandans, but have I experienced the reality of this life? Can I really know what it's like?

I have not truly felt the oppression of chronic malnutrition and sickness, of the lack of certain school facilities and the poor quality of others, of the need to spend hours collecting firewood or water that may not be safe to drink, or of finding very limited opportunities for employment. These are situations that can trap people in cycles of poverty, through no fault of their own. Having not fallen into this spiral myself, I may not be able to claim that I know what people are going through every day, despite my physical nearness to the causes and symptoms. I could, perhaps, explain the issues and how they can arise, but I can't begin to describe how they affect someone mentally and emotionally. I can't say how it might create a sense of hopelessness, or how it might cause someone to lose faith in others who come in, trying to help, with a limited understanding of the situation.

It is sometimes hard to remember that I am unlikely to fathom the deepest feelings and frustrations weighing on another's soul. It is easy to become frustrated, myself, when others shun an idea that seems like common sense to me. It's easy to forget that every person has an untold story, informing reactions to others and to the outside world.

I hope that the work I am doing with Brick by Brick is making a small impact, that we are doing a little bit to improve lives and to ensure a measure of long-term progress and sustainability. But, can I really understand how someone's life might be changed, when I haven't lived that life myself? I may be able to see certain physical changes, but emotional and mental changes, for better or worse, are less visible. And these are, perhaps, more important. The most crucial work must be done, and is being done, by people with this understanding. It is being done by Ugandans, whose hopes lie within themselves, who have faith in their abilities and their goals, and who believe that they and their neighbors deserve healthy lives full of opportunity, promise, and love.

Their voices are so important. I may be able to provide some sense of local circumstances, especially for people in other countries who never have the chance to come here and see. The full story, however, can only be discovered if the people living in these circumstances are able to speak, and if their voices are able to be heard. Only then can the fantasies and fairy tales be identified for what they are.

I'm reminded of a process that began last year, as a result of a seemingly small statement made by a female student at one of Brick by Brick's partner schools. She mentioned to one of the women on our staff that, as older girls begin to go through puberty, it becomes harder for them to stay in school. One of the major reasons involves menstruation. Along with the stigma commonly associated with this natural part of life, many girls and their families cannot afford disposable sanitary pads, so they use pieces of cloth, toilet paper, or other similar materials. When attending school during a menstrual period, girls face additional challenges. School latrines are often in poor condition, and it can be difficult or impossible to find much-needed privacy. As a result, many girls are faced with feelings of shame and embarrassment, leading some to skip school and some to drop out entirely.

This concern was a new one for Brick by Brick as an organization, but, from this one student's fervent desire to stay in school and to find a better way to deal with the issue, a new program was born. My coworkers began to do some research, conducted needs assessments in local schools, and talked to other organizations and volunteers who were working to address this topic. A number of Peace Corps Volunteers and their Ugandan coworkers had put together educational materials concerning reproductive health and reusable menstrual pads that girls and women could make using locally available materials. Our staff worked with other volunteers to adapt these materials for Brick by Brick.

In the end, they created what I think is a very appropriate and important program that includes a number of educational sessions for both female and male students, discussing puberty and reproductive health. The program also contains sessions where students and teachers learn how to make their own reusable menstrual pads. Brick by Brick calls it the My Pad Program, and Suzan is in the process of conducting the first few sessions in the first few schools right now. The hope is that, in time, it can be expanded to more schools, where it will enable more students to have access to this program.

All of it was made possible by the seemingly small voice of one young person, who had been brave enough to speak, almost a year before, about an issue that affected her and others she knew. There is strength in that, a slow-growing strength with the power to change lives as it spreads.

The Strength within the Smallest Voice

Silence! For someone is speaking.
Hearken, to hearts quickly beating.
Faintly, the floorboards are creaking,
Swelling, with soft truth so fleeting.

She stands upon the strange, cold stage,
So new, so shy, so young of age.
Her slender voice betrays her fear,
As she describes the fateful cage
Of cruel, impoverished life so near.
She lives it, and she sees it clear;
And those who hear her honest voice,
They name their future silence fear.

Silence! But some there are seeking.
Hearken, to hearts now repeating,
Faintly, the fledgling drop, leaking,
Swelling, in streams not retreating.

Her voice is guiding through the night,
And showing us the shattered height
Of unknown neighbors' unreached dreams
And systems that obscure their light;
And though a drop within the streams
Is all, to some, she humbly seems,
This drop could lead a peaceful flow
To change the unjust status quo.

Then all may love and truly live,
For all the power greed can give
Won't stop a multitude's fair choice,
The strength within the smallest voice.

Too often, perhaps, we hear stories about what certain groups, organizations, or countries have done for those in Africa, for those seen as less fortunate. I feel like this kind of language puts the focus in the wrong place altogether. So many ideas, so much progress, so much initiative comes from those so-called less fortunate people themselves. I know, in my case, I wouldn't be able to do much of anything that's appropriate and lasting if I did not have dedicated Ugandans working beside me.

At this point, Brick by Brick has three core staff members working in its office: Suzan, Prossy, and Max. These are the people in Kalisizo to whom I have grown closest, and each one of them is a hardworking, devoted, and kind individual. Suzan coordinates the My Pad Program and conducts health and hygiene trainings in local schools and communities. She is also a trained midwife and works in the Kalisizo Hospital. I don't know the exact number of babies she has delivered, but she has certainly been there at the beginning of the lives of many people living in this area. In the mornings, before coming to work at Brick by Brick or at the hospital, she spends some time farming at her house, which is a few minutes outside of town. Unfortunately, her husband passed away several years ago, and she is working to put her children through college. I know that she has been trying to secure scholarships for her twin girls, so that they can attend a local university. She puts in long hours every day to bring about a better life for her children, and she is one of the kindest and most steadfast people I have ever met.

Prossy is Brick by Brick's office administrator. She has experience with accounting, marketing, and business development, and she is certainly the most comfortable on the computer. She has been a big help to Suzan and Max, who do a great job interacting with local communities, but who may not yet have the technical expertise to compose an electronic report or create a complex spreadsheet. They are getting better, for sure, but Prossy is our master in these areas. Prossy lives in town with her husband and their young children. Actually, she also owns the restaurant where we usually eat lunch. Early in the morning, she is busy getting things started at the restaurant and raising her chickens, which are another source of income for her and her family.

Prossy loves to laugh, and she always brightens our day in the office. Just a few days ago, she enjoyed surprising me with a plate of cooked grasshoppers while we were eating lunch. Right now, it's the season when the grasshoppers are out, and all sorts of people set up apparatuses to collect them. The common method involves positioning fifty-gallon drums beneath bright lights attached to wooden poles. Long, corrugated metal sheets are placed inside the drums so that they extend upward, stopping just beneath the lights. At night, the grasshoppers are attracted by the lights, crashing into them. They fall onto the sheets and slide down into the drums, where they can be collected in the morning. Electricity becomes even more uncertain during this season, as grasshopper collectors put together dubious wiring schemes to power these islands of light in the dark seas of the night. Local residents do not seem to mind, though. Most enjoy the final product, after the grasshoppers are fried. They are actually pretty tasty.

In any case, Prossy and Suzan are two strong and dedicated women who are very special to me, and my experience would be completely different without them. But, with Max, I think my relationship is a bit different. When I was just beginning my time in Kalisizo, it was often just the two of us in that office, and we worked very closely with one another for long hours every day. I did not have a great deal of work experience before coming to Uganda, but I've never had a closer working relationship with anyone. Max is about thirty years my senior, and, during our time together, we have developed something of a father and son relationship. I sometimes feel as if I am a part of his family.

In addition to being Brick by Brick's program coordinator – which means that he is primarily responsible for most, if not all, of the organization's projects and programs – Max is also extremely involved in the local Catholic church. He lives in Kajaguzo, a village a few kilometers away from Kalisizo, where he helped to start a primary school for local children. His wife, Teddy, teaches at that school, and, along with their own children, they have also taken in orphans and others from the area.

It's hard to believe that, in addition to grasshopper season, it's also Christmas season. It certainly doesn't feel like it, with no snow, no cold, and no overwhelming array of department store advertisements. Instead of chestnuts roasting on an open fire, we have grasshoppers drying in the sun. This will be my second Christmas in this country, and, as I think about Max, I recall the first.

Only a few months into my service, Max invited me to spend that first Christmas with his family in Kajaguzo. At that point, I was not sure if I would take him up on his offer. I had hoped to travel to see some other volunteers over the holiday, and I had been a bit frustrated with Max for the past few weeks. Among other things, his timeliness had seemed to be getting less and less reliable, and I felt like I needed a break from the stress of our work. I later discovered that, around this time, Max's mother had taken a turn for the worse. She had been living with him and his family as her health gradually declined, and it seemed that the decline had begun to move more quickly.

One evening, as I was cooking dinner in my house, I got a call from Max. Wondering what could be so urgent that he would call me so late, I answered, and I heard Max say, "John, my mother has died."

"Oh, Max, I'm so sorry," I replied, taken aback.

"Thank you," he said sadly, and the call was over.

The next day, I rode my bike through the dusty, uneven paths, suffering a flat tire on the way, to reach Kajaguzo and Max's house. I found him outside with a number of other men, engaging in subdued conversation and preparing for the night. After someone passes away, close friends and family come to the house and sleep outside, usually under a tarp. Over the next few days, culminating in a funeral at the home of Max's brother, we spent quite a bit of time together, and I realized how petty my previous frustrations truly were.

During the funeral itself, I was not able to interact with Max very much. Instead, I spent most of my time with a teacher from Kajaguzo's primary school, who seemed to enjoy explaining the ceremony to me and asking me how it worked in the United States. When I arrived, lunch was being served, and a Catholic mass followed. All the while, several men were working in a nearby field, digging the grave where Max's mother would be placed. When all was ready, she was carried to the grave, wrapped in a burial shroud. As the ceremony came to an end, in the confusion of the dispersing crowd, I found Max and told him that I would like to spend Christmas with him and his family. His face seemed to brighten slightly, as he replied, "Oh, wonderful! Let me go tell Teddy."

And so, my first Christmas in Uganda was spent in Kajaguzo, with Max, Teddy, and their children. It was a crowded house – larger than mine, but still quite small when accommodating over ten people. I slept in a modest, yet comfortable bed in a tiny corner room, and there was little for me to do. No one seemed to want me, the guest, to do anything. I had not even brought a book to read, so I spent a few days simply being with this family. We ate – a lot. Teddy served huge plates full of *matooke*, *posho*, rice, beans, cabbage, and beef for Christmas dinner, all of which had been cooked in a little structure separated from the main house. Many of the ingredients came straight from the family's gardens. Max and I spent afternoons meandering through those gardens, walking around the village, and visiting some of his friends. In the evenings, the kids fired up a diesel generator so that we could watch movies on a tiny television set in the house's largest room, where the walls were lined with pictures of family members, positioned above large couches and cushioned chairs. The adults drank bottles of warm beer, taken from a crate kept in the corner, while the children drank warm soda.

For the most part, those few days were subdued and thoroughly relaxing. There were no decorations. We sang no carols. We decorated no tree. We exchanged no gifts, although Max was curious to learn about who this Santa Claus character is. We had only the small blessings that anyone is capable of sharing – our time and ourselves. We were just a simple family, being together, and it felt right.

All That's Left is Right

In Matthew, we start out to find
A kingly genealogy,
The words of scriptures past outlined,
Fulfillment of the prophecy,
Joseph's angelic dream recalled,
His choice to stay with Mary,
Eastern Magi, a star they saw,
And royal gifts they carried.

In Luke, a detailed long account
Reveals a physician's mind,
A mother releases any doubt,
Her holy task defined,

In Bethlehem, King David's town,
No room for two or three,
And shepherds hear the angels' sound,
Far from royalty.

In Mark, the shortest of the four,
The birth remains unmentioned,
Baptism, rather, opens the door,
To capture the earth's attention,
While John's majestic opening
Of light and truth and love,
Reveals for this small baby boy
An eternity above.

The joyful tale we know so well
That comes with each December
Takes more than one to fully tell,
So perhaps we should remember,
Peace on earth, good will to all,
One viewpoint may not bring,
Instead, we might tear down the wall,
To hear as others sing.

The tales, like us, when stripped to the core,
Show something that's the same,
Whether one is rich or poor,
Regardless of one's name.
Beyond the trees, the turtledoves,
The tinsel, and the light,
Left with new life's hope and love,
All that's left is right.

There's more to this story, isn't there? To feel the full effect, to touch all of the details, we need to experience a variety of accounts, a variety of perspectives. The Christmas story is not complete if we read only one version, just as this life is not complete if we limit ourselves to only one perspective. Our relationships, our connections to others, provide us with a broader view.

If nothing else, the past year has humbled me. I've discovered that

I cannot operate as if I live in a place where all of my ideas and ideals are true. An important part of living in this world involves the fact that all of our thoughts do not line up. While it is good to work toward our ideals, that happens within a community of individuals who are similar, yet unique. We are connected to one another, but the combination of experiences, beliefs, thoughts, and actions that comprises one person is distinct and valuable. We need to remain open to hearing the voices of others, especially those who may appear to be more widely separated from us. Those voices may open our eyes to circumstances we never knew existed. Those voices are dear.

To some degree, is that not what makes our lives and our world so interesting and charming? We know that we are not perfect, that we cannot do everything ourselves, that we don't have all the answers. No one is pure light or pure darkness. We are all some shade of gray. The imperfections, the inconsistencies, the mental battles within ourselves, the uncertainties – these are what make us human, and these are what make those brief glimpses, when perspectives coalesce and the universe seems to work together in harmony, all the more beautiful.

I know now that I am not here shining a light in the darkness. Light surrounds me. I am not here to lift these people up from their misery, to give hope to the hopeless. They have hope. They don't need me to give them hope. They need me, and I need them, simply because we all need each other. I am here to work with them as equals, bringing in a different viewpoint and different skills, to try to make a small portion of all our hopes a reality. You don't need to thank me for my sacrifice. I am here because I want to be here. Light is all around me, and I just hope that my own light can contribute to the whole.

And I believe it can, even in the smallest of ways. A few months after that first Christmas spent in Kajaguzo, Max and Teddy asked me to go with them to visit Patrick – their son, twelve years old at the time – at his boarding school. Patrick and I had already developed a fairly close relationship. When he was not away at school, he would bike over to my house on the weekends, we would talk for a bit, and then, with my laptop, I would teach him a little about how to use a computer. When school was in session, he would spend months away from his family. At his age, I could not imagine going to boarding

63

school, but, in Uganda, if a family can find the money, as many children as possible are sent there. In terms of infrastructure and general quality, these private schools are usually far above the level of their public counterparts.

So, on the school's designated Visitation Day, we spent a day with Patrick, meeting with his teachers, seeing his classrooms, and hearing a speech from the school's head teacher. Honestly, it was not the most exciting day, but it was nice to see Patrick and to know that he is doing well. After we returned to Kalisizo, as I was saying good night and thanking Max and Teddy for asking me to join them, Max said, "Thank you for the friendship you have shown today."

It was a striking statement, reminding me that something small can mean a great deal to others. I certainly did not start the day thinking that tagging along with the family would be a big deal, but Max and Teddy seemed to appreciate it quite a bit. A small voice, a small action, can make all the difference.

I know that I need that small, supportive voice every so often as well, as I face difficulties and discover that my responses are rarely perfect. Whatever troubles arise during the day, I often find that simple support when I come home after work and see the little kids in my compound. They don't care what mistakes I may have made that day. If they know, they seem to let it go quickly.

There is one little girl, Ashley, who is two or three years old. For the past month, her mom has been persuading her to greet me whenever I arrive. Her mom tells her to ask, "How are you?" to which I reply, "I'm fine, how are you?" Then her mom encourages her to say, "I'm okay." She has a long way to go before she gets the pronunciation right, but she's started to do it without prompting. A few days ago, I stepped outside of my house while Ashley was crying about something. I wasn't feeling that great either. When she saw me, she suddenly got quiet, concentrated for a second, and then asked, "Ah bah boo?"

"I'm fine," I replied with a smile. And I was. One voice is all it takes.

One Solitary Candle

One solitary candle sits
In a decaying, darkened house,

64

Sits in a jar of broken glass,
As its flame consumes the past.
Layers of last night's hardened wax
Left to rest upon the bottom,
As this night's liquid hourglass
Drips slowly down the mast,
Yet still too fast it seems to him,
Who waits inside the window,
Left to face what comes to pass
Alone in darkness vast.

He waits for you, who comes on wings
Of steady, relentless time,
For you, who comes for all at last
At this cold hour's chime.

One solitary candle sits
Then softly flickers out,
A waxy pool the only sign
Of what your breeze put out.

"Alas," I said, "he finds his peace,"
But the breeze then whispered low:
"His final night not quite so bleak,
If you had stopped and said hello."

MOVEMENT 6 | DREAMING

In the Stillness of the Night

In the stillness of the night,
One pin is as a rock,
One bird may seem a flock,
One thought may be a shock,
In the stillness of the night.

In the absence of the light,
One tap is as a gun,
One flame may seem a sun,
One presence here may stun,
In the absence of the light.

In the silence of our plight,
One word is as a plea,
One drop may seem a sea,
One love envelops me,
In the silence of our plight.

In the stillness of the night,
Where nothing seems to come to light
But the sadness of our plight,
There you're found to fill the soul aright,
In the stillness of the night.

The electricity is out tonight. It has been out for almost a week, and I have been carefully rationing the limited battery power I have left in my computer, so that I can use it to get a bit more work done tomorrow. After more than a year and a half, I am used to the problems that come with unreliable electricity, but the apparently random moments when everything suddenly goes dark – when the drone of local carpentry and metal shops is silenced, when the music from the bar down the road stops playing, and when the entire town releases a collective sigh of resignation – continue to irritate me and try my patience.

Usually, the power is only out for a few hours. Sometimes, it cuts off for nearly an entire day. Once in a great while, an outage will extend across several days. When larger towns experience these difficulties, nearly all of the businesses and shops will pull out generators, and the entire town will be filled with the harsh, clamorous hum of diesel power. In Kalisizo, a few of the gas stations, internet cafés, and welding shops might turn on their generators, but, for the most part, the town experiences a hushed stillness.

Especially at night, everything seems a bit more peaceful. Sitting here, surrounded by darkness, reading and writing by the light of a single candle placed just inside the window, a sense of calm seems to enter the room and wrap me in its embrace. Stepping outside, smelling the grass beneath my feet, feeling the cool evening breeze blowing across my face and through the leaves of nearby trees, hearing the ensemble of insects and other nocturnal creatures as they serenade the stars, it's almost magical. I suppose that it's probably much easier to enjoy the night and feel its beauty, living in a place where so many nights throughout the year have the character of a gentle, mildly warm midsummer evening, but I can't help thinking that something apart from climate attracts me to this time.

During these hours, my sense of sight is hindered, but other senses become heightened as I accept that fact. The past few nights, as my solitary candle flickered out, I have sat on the floor in silence, eyes closed, and have marveled at the music all around me, music that often goes unnoticed when other thoughts are flying through my mind. There are mysterious melodies in the breeze as it whispers through the trees, strange songs that vaguely flutter on the wings of the crickets and the birds. I hear them more clearly now that my mind has been quieted by the slower and softer pace of a life without light bulbs and charging cords.

For the past several weeks, I have been trying to meditate each night, just before I go to sleep. When I started, my hope was that this practice would still my mind and help to improve my patience during the day. What I found was a mental restlessness that was, for a long time, nearly impossible to quiet. I have an active mind, which is pushed to be even more dynamic as I undergo the tumultuous process of trying to reconcile my nights with my days, of trying to join the person I want to be and the ideals contained in my dreams with the person I am and the realities I see in the light of day. I find myself trying, sometimes in vain, to piece together the disparate influences of the darkness and the light, both of which have something valuable to contribute.

But, in these past few evenings of greater stillness, my thoughts are released and my mind is set free. It reaches out to the surrounding air, discovering those subtle melodies that resonate within neighboring life, and it feels the connections that can only be discerned when the external senses are dimmed and the inner soul expands outward. It is in these moments that I feel a sustaining and enduring presence that passes through each life, solidifying, deepening, and enriching those connections. Somewhere beneath the surface of the mind, in the subconscious currents of half-dreams and unclear hopes, where thought no longer depends on reasoned logic and where leaps of insight too profound for words can be made, I come upon a foundation of goodness and truth, from which the diverse streams of life originate in unity, and to which they return in the end. In that fundamental substance is the touch of serenity.

Serenity

Softly and gently lies the quiet night
Upon the enchanted, gray-green earth.
Slowly and simply, I feel it invite,
Enclosing my mind with its worth,
Kneeling in sacred contemplation,
Drifting deep in meditation.

Calmly and coolly join the silent streams
As I have done countless times before.

Lightly and lazily, floating on dreams,
So easy to once more restore,
But something whispers faint in my mind,
Warnings of pride, deeply entwined.

Haughtily, heavily, wandering thought
Allows subtle noise to envelop,
Quickly, chaotically, worries are brought,
Quivering as they develop.
Internal ear hears their frenzied flow,
Questions of past and tomorrow.

Loudly and lamely, I shout forth with pride,
Though lost in this sea of muted sound.
Actually, achingly, needing a guide,
My focus has fled and been drowned,
Thinking, still, I might salvage, but no,
Caught in this sinking undertow.

Humbly and heavily, feeble and blind,
Coming to rest on the soft seafloor,
Soberly sorry for my frantic mind,
Your help, from within, I implore,
Then rising to rest on calm, cool shores,
I know it forever endures.

Whispers of the trees, ballads in the breeze
Softly and gently lead me to see,
In my headstrong search for peace I could seize,
Serenity simply found me.

And yet, how does one reconcile the basic goodness I feel beneath all existence with the obstinate and debilitating evil so often thrust into being? Countless examples of pain and suffering can be found throughout the world. One instance that hits close to my current home is the Rwandan genocide of 1994.

Rwanda has made great progress in the years since that deadly horror. At the same time, evidence of the genocide can today be found in Uganda. Last week, I visited a fishing village on Lake

Victoria. To reach it, we traveled south on the main road towards Tanzania, and then turned left onto a dirt road that crossed thickly vegetated hills and valleys until it arrived at the lake. Along the right side of this road, near the top of a hill, we came across a burial site of over 2,800 victims of the Rwandan genocide. We learned that, after a mass killing in Rwanda, the bodies were dumped into the Kagera River, which flows from the Rwandan border, through Tanzania, and into Lake Victoria at the southern end of Uganda. The bodies floated the whole way to the lake, where they were found and brought to this site for burial.

To be sure, the occurrence and impact of evil are not confined to countries in Africa or to other parts of the world that some consider to be less developed. Evil is not only present in the mass murder of thousands of people. It can also be found in smaller, individual acts and, perhaps, in some of the underlying structures of societies themselves, although these instances are more difficult to clearly see.

I find myself returning to perpetual questions I am never able to answer. How can we do this to one another? How can we treat other human beings with such callous disregard for compassion, humanity, or even life itself? How is it possible for one group of people to feel so far removed from another group that they are able to take away thousands of lives? Perhaps the most frightening question of all: What would I have done if I were placed somewhere in this type of situation? The repeated horrors of history seem to suggest that we all have the potential, somewhere inside of us, to participate in brutal atrocities or to silently stand by and watch as they occur.

Do these questions have answers? It all seems so inexplicable. What conditions, what circumstances, what accepted lies can lead us to see no problem in killing another? I was in the latrine a few nights ago, and, in a corner between the wall and the door, I saw a fly get caught in a spider's web. As the spider went over to make sure the fly didn't escape, I found myself feeling sorry for the fly. A spider killing a fly so that it can eat and survive is drastically different from one human being killing another human being because he can. But, if we have the capacity to sympathize with an insect as it dies, how can we also have the capacity to begin to see other human beings as bugs that must be crushed? And yet, it happens. Mass killings, genocides, and wars occur, and maybe I am capable of terrible things too. I have not experienced it, thankfully, and, at least at this point, I cannot understand it.

Maybe that's right. Maybe we're not supposed to understand it. Maybe we were meant for something more, something higher, something that is so different from oppression, torture, and killing that these evils should be incomprehensible. Over the past week, as I have spent part of my evenings struggling with these questions, something different has dawned on me in the darkness of the night. I've started getting into the habit, right before meditating and then going to bed, of stepping outside, just to look up at the sky and take in all of the stars. Especially on nights when the power is out, I can see so many stars, just by walking out my door. It's absolutely beautiful, and it reminds me of our true situation in this universe. We are so very, very small. I am looking up at millions and millions of tiny lights that are actually massive stars, similar to our own sun, which is many times larger than our little blue planet. And those are just the stars I can see from here. There are millions more out there in our galaxy, which is just one of many galaxies in the universe. And here we are, a tiny speck in the midst of it all.

Does that mean that everything here is inconsequential, that any amount of pain and suffering is insignificant? No, each life has meaning and is important. What I take from our smallness in a vast universe is that the infinitely complex interactions of chance and choice contribute to create bad, even terrible situations in some parts of this universe at certain points in time. Some of these situations may be completely inexplicable, but they do not endure forever. The constant pattern of change that runs through the universe cannot wash away each person's individual suffering, but it might suggest that things could get better. The bedrock of goodness underpinning the universe is itself infinitely larger than we are and is present in the midst of these difficult situations, working through the souls of those living within them. It is here, at the interface, that evil might be transformed into something else entirely.

The Interface

The darkness rises
As our light begins to die.
Pain's cry reprises,
Never understanding why,

71

But deprivations that the soul despises
Reveal you in humanity's disguises.
When the earth may bleed into the sky,
At the interface your love will lie.

On the surface of the universe, we see death, destruction, suffering, and war, and it becomes easy to wonder what kind of horrible force is behind it all. But in looking deeper, in seeing past the surface, in considering the basic building blocks of the universe, I find something wholly different.

At some point a long time ago, atoms and molecules that had not been alive were somehow drawn together to create life, generating a concentrated patch of order from a sea of growing disorder. The process of creating life goes against the general current of decay and deterioration that seems to define the universe as time marches onward, and it is to this process, which creates organisms that are far more than the sum of their parts, that we owe our entire existence and so much of the beauty within that existence.

The creation of life is somehow connected with love. Whatever the ambiguities of this life are, the effects of love are clear, and I have seen and learned so many of them in this place. Love creates bonds of friendship. It forms communities. Even new life can spring from our expressions of love. Love builds. It brings together, creating order, purpose, and meaning out of chaos and disorder. The expression of love and the creation of life have similar qualities. The creation of life constitutes the origin of our existence, and love is there with it.

How does it all relate? Why, when I stand outside and lift my eyes to the sky, do I feel drawn to the stars? Part of it might be that I am attracted by ideas of scientific exploration and discovery. Another part of it might be that I see a greater opening to philosophical contemplation within the night sky. Always, it connects to an innate desire to know more about myself and about my place in the universe. Is it possible that we on this planet have a direct connection with the stars themselves? In other words, by knowing more about these stars and what they are, can we learn something about ourselves?

Early on in the life of the universe, subatomic particles combined to form hydrogen, the smallest element. Through the attractive force of gravity, hydrogen atoms came together, forming clouds that eventually collapsed into stars, fueled by nuclear fusion, in which hydrogen atoms fuse together to create larger helium atoms and produce huge amounts of energy. As those stars aged, larger atoms, like carbon, oxygen, nitrogen, and calcium, were created. Finally, when certain stars died, those various elements shot out into the expanse of space to find a new home. In other words, the building blocks of life on this planet were born, long ago and far away, in a distant star. The atoms of which we and everything in this world are made can trace their lineage back across a vast series of moments to remote places and times.

So, in the middle of the night, I look up to those stars, and I feel a connection between my inner soul and the outermost reaches of the universe. A star is something more to me than a huge, isolated, flaming ball. There is more to us, and more to the universe around us, than we can observe with our senses or even, perhaps, measure with the incredibly complex scientific instruments generated by our collective knowledge. From deep within our souls, beyond the reach of the intellect, we search for the thing we feel but cannot pinpoint. We search for the potential to be more than what we are now.

These connections and impressions are not easy to explain. How can I be intimately connected to distant points in the universe? To me, possible explanations must transcend our limited conceptions of physical reality and float through higher dimensions.

According to our senses, physical reality is composed of three spatial dimensions and one temporal dimension. Certain theories in physics, however, postulate that a number of other dimensions are also present, going in directions that we cannot physically comprehend. In a similar vein, but acknowledging that I am moving completely into the realm of speculation, what if I were to suggest the existence of a spiritual dimension? Knowing that it involves a significant leap of faith, could all of these ideas surrounding the relationship between life and love, as well as the foundation of goodness that resides beneath the surface of the universe, be combined into one overarching system? Realizing that another leap of belief is required, can this presence of goodness and love, this center from which life springs, be called God?

In my mind, to make this possibility easier to visualize in three dimensions, I often simplify the physical space of the universe down to a two-dimensional surface. For example, the surface of a sphere is two-dimensional, in that any point confined to the surface can only move in some combination of two directions: latitude and longitude, like a ship on the sea. The surface of the sphere represents the material universe, and points on the surface represent us, along with other physical things present in the universe. Now, if we take the inside of the sphere, along the radius, to represent an additional spiritual dimension, with God at the center, maybe we can begin to understand how this system might work.

As material beings, our physical movement is restricted to the sphere's surface, but our existence also has a spiritual dimension to it. Each of our souls functions as the intersection between these two realms, the material and spiritual, springing out of their interaction. Our link to the spiritual can be strengthened by how we live, enabling divine goodness and love to break into the material world through each of us. Perhaps the most obvious way to connect ourselves with the spiritual involves developing a bond with God. The radius of the sphere can be drawn from its center to any point on the surface, meaning that every point is linked to the center. Different people form this bond in different ways. For me, I think it usually involves some combination of music, service, and personal reflection.

A direct connection to the center is not the only way this link is solidified. The loving relationships we develop with one another can also contribute. For any two points on the curved surface, a straight line joining them would travel inside the sphere. In other words, the connection has a spiritual component, as well as a material one. Perhaps this bond can then coalesce with each point's link to the center, creating a circuit of positive feedback. Is this what it means to see through the heart, to recognize God in others? If so, it provides a window into our purpose, showing us why we are important to the overall equation. God's love is made complete and can be fully expressed through us and through the rest of the world.

To be sure, this system may be a relatively complex way of conceptualizing the interaction between the physical and spiritual sides of ourselves. Others undoubtedly have alternative strategies for fathoming these ideas, ideas which are far beyond our complete comprehension. Each perspective can perhaps better illuminate different aspects of the divine. For me, the model in my head has certain qualities that help me to see what I think are important themes of life. It shows the vast, complex web of interconnectedness that characterizes our existence. If we have links, however thin and far removed, with distant points in the universe, then how much more closely are we related to each other? We are profoundly interdependent on one another. The spiritual and physical well-being of someone else can have an impact on my own. Do I live my life with that in mind? Do we use that awareness for good?

This is not simply a personal philosophy that applies only to my individual spiritual life. It is comprehensive. It evokes a way of living, with real and active social dimensions. It suggests the preeminence of relationships. It implies the importance of reaching out to those who are oppressed, marginalized, and perceived as outcasts, and hearing their voices.

The Center of the Universal Sphere

Somewhere clear of the confines of time,
Outside the gaze of the stars,
None hears the sound of the midnight chime,
Or sees the face full of scars.
Space and time as we know them to be,
At that point, they pass away,
While the triumphs and trials of life are set free,
And perceived in a different way.

Is it true, what I hear, that none sheds a tear
In the center of the universal sphere?

On the surface, the sphere, full of spirit and thought,
Holds the realm of our waking eyes,
Where something like love can be sold or bought
Or sunk in a lake of lies.
One cannot dismiss this plane's imperfection,
Yet good could still be supplied,
On the surface is space for expression, through action,
Of spirit-touched love from inside.

Each soul, it seems clear, as a cross could appear,
At which matter and spirit cohere.

Surface points on the sphere, irrespective of kind,
Can exhibit each component quality.
In the physical plane, spatial form one will find,
In the radius, spiritual beauty.
But greatest value will come from the two vectors' sum,
And connecting one's own to others',
For no fortunes or doctrines or dogmas should come
Before love for life's sisters and brothers.

Touching points there and here, inner lines will draw near
To the center of the universal sphere.

The shortest distance to steer through two points on an arc
Is a line cutting inside the curve.
Tensile force then pulls points toward the central mark
And fires a spiritual nerve.
These lines show relations of peace and equality
Among people and all of existence,
A jointly-formed filter to reduce the turbidity
That clouds the spiritual substance.

And in a soul's final year, when matter's ties disappear,
Could connections pull it into the sphere?

But what of the tear about which there was query
Whether ever it falls in the core?
Now I cannot be sure, but I present here a theory
Based on that which has come before.
There are those who do not form connections of peace,
Of love, equality, or kindness.
Instead they pursue, seeming never to cease,
Means to power, to wealth, and to blindness.
Some prey on those whom they see as below them,
Or those who seem not quite the same,
While some, solely fixed on a goal or a gem,
Are unmoved by those losing the game.
But although they may gain all the things they have sought,
Time fades power and fine, precious stone.
The permanent value of love they have not,
Without connection, souls drift off alone.

So perhaps, a soft tear, for these souls, will appear,
And for those whose connections they shear.

But let us be clear, yes, let us remember,
These sad souls are not simply "they".
In each of us fidgets a flickering ember,
That burns our connections away.
Yet, in all of us, also, a stream from the center
Supports and joins one to another.
All we need do is allow it to enter,
To flow, and the flames it will smother.

So join hands without fear, and together draw near
To the center of the universal sphere.

Let me not be disingenuous. These spiritual ideas did not develop safely, slowly, and steadily over the past one and a half years. They grew in fits and starts, with significant periods of doubt, uncertainty, and skepticism in between. And, even though they begin to establish for me a way of thinking about the relationships that connect us to God and to the surrounding universe, they are certainly not complete or fully conceived. This system is imperfect, as is any attempt to comprehend the infinite intricacy of the spiritual and physical realms, and it paints in broad strokes. It still remains for me or others to identify the finer points contained within. This journey of discovery is far from over.

Last month, I found myself being questioned about my journey of faith. Max and I were visiting a local complex that functions as both a Christian church and a school, discussing with the staff there the possibility of doing some construction work at the site. For a few minutes, Max walked off with a few of the staff people to talk about the details of the work, and I ended up talking one-on-one with a woman who teaches at the complex and helps it run. The conversation, as so often happens in Uganda, turned to my religion. Usually, the fact that I have been a Christian all my life makes these moments relatively easy to handle. Christianity is the religion practiced by most Ugandans, while Muslims constitute a smaller, but still substantial, fraction of the country's population. Generally speaking, followers of these two faith traditions are accepting of one another, and we in the United States might learn something from their tolerance. At any rate, my identification as a Christian can often help to create a sense of commonality between me and those around me. However, for other volunteers who follow traditions that are less locally familiar, and especially for those who identify as atheists or agnostics, these conversations concerning religion can become more difficult and awkward.

In this specific case, though, my own conversation quickly became difficult as well. After explaining that I had grown up in a Christian family, that we attended church nearly every Sunday, and that I had continued to be active in religious groups throughout college, I was asked if I am "born again". I balked at this question. That phrase always causes me to stop. I don't think it accurately describes my own journey of faith. I have experienced a number of what I would call spiritual awakenings in my life, but they are never final. They always leave more to be learned. Perhaps it is an incorrect understanding of the phrase, but, to me, the words "born again" suggest a specific date in one's life at which faith's search stops. Across the changing moments of my life, I can say with nearly complete certainty that I will be searching, asking questions, and exploring new perspectives until I die. God will always be bigger than my own conception of the divine, so my search continues. I cannot pinpoint one single moment of "new birth". If I were to attempt to use the given analogy, perhaps I would say that, along with several spiritual valleys and depressions, I have gone through and will undergo hundreds of incremental spiritual births, rebirths, and awakenings throughout my life.

Unfortunately, my mind usually does not work so quickly in the heat of the moment, and none of these ideas were given voice. Instead, I found myself hesitating and stuttering, struggling to find words that could express the initial seeds of these thoughts, which were only more fully conceived much later. Those moments of hesitation were taken as an implied "no", and my companion stated, quite matter-of-factly, that I was not a true Christian. I realize that the way I think about spiritual matters may be slightly unconventional, but I had never before encountered this charge.

Revisiting this statement now, though, I must acknowledge that there have been periods in my life when I have struggled with serious spiritual doubts and questions. Before coming to Uganda, the most significant strain on my faith often reared its head during those service trips to Nicaragua, as I grappled with questions of suffering and evil. After seeing so much pain in the lives of innocent people, I asked how a loving God could allow these conditions. This question has been explored by a vast array of thinkers throughout history, offering solutions or responses of varying worth and plausibility. Some people are led to abandon a belief in God as a result of this question. I feel the weight of these issues and can understand this decision. However, after spending a substantial amount of time thinking and considering the assorted arguments, my own response was not to reject God. I have come to believe that God does not control events like some eternal puppet master. Through the forces of free will and choice (which can easily give rise to personal, social, and structural corruption in a world of imperfect beings), as well as the influence of blind chance (which science suggests is a key component of the universe at the subatomic level), evils falling outside the realm of God's love and goodness inevitably occur. I look for God in the midst of the suffering, working in the hearts of the peacemakers, the caretakers, and the victims.

While those challenges have surfaced again in Uganda, I have found new questions as well. The most significant of these issues includes three elements. First, I look at my friends in the Peace Corps. They are certainly a religiously diverse group, and each person has his or her own motivations for serving. My faith certainly played some role in getting me to this point, but, for others, that may not have been the case. As different as everyone is, all are wonderful and compassionate people – many probably more so than me – and the reasons behind their service are no less valid than my own.

My mind turns from these people to the Bible sitting on top of the small set of shelves in my bedroom. I have read every word in that book. I think of the strong moral and ethical teachings that helped lead me toward the Peace Corps, but I also think of fantastical, almost unbelievable events and accounts of atrocities committed in the name of God. I have to acknowledge that a good deal of logical and historical baggage is entangled in this faith.

I turn once again and consider some of the current applications of the faith. I see Christians pronouncing judgment on various groups and individuals as if it were the word of God. I see churches forgetting to love the oppressed and marginalized sitting on their doorstep, apparently more concerned with other issues. I consider these elements, and I wonder if the positive offerings of Christianity are worth the negative connotations associated with it.

I know that I am far from perfect. I'm not appointed to pass judgment – I don't even attend church here in Uganda. Apart from a few weekends spent with Max's family, when I have gone with them to a Catholic church near their village, my Sundays are normally reserved for reading, working, or relaxing. During training, my excuse was that I was so exhausted by the time Sunday rolled around, and I needed a day to sleep in and recover. I could use the same excuse now, in Kalisizo, but, to be completely honest, I just don't have the desire to go while I'm here. Part of it is due to language. All of the churches in Kalisizo worship in Luganda, not in English. While I might be able to pick out some words and maybe even understand the larger ideas from time to time, it is exhausting, and I find myself more concerned with the exercise of translation than with considering the actual content and having any sort of meaningful worship experience.

After a life in which church services always played a key role, not going to church is, perhaps, allowing me to step back and take a more objective view. In the end, despite its human flaws and serious imperfections, I think that Christianity does still have something valuable to say. It has something to say about humbly acknowledging our faults, our limitations, and the fact that we don't fully understand God or the divine will. It has something to say about putting the needs of others above our own. It has something to say about hearing the voices of the oppressed, the marginalized, and the outcasts – about reaching out to them and working together to make this world a more equal and just place for everyone.

This is who I am trying to become. These are the words I am trying to say: I have faith, but unanswered questions will continue leading me to search for a higher – yet always insufficient – level of understanding. I am far from perfect, but, like the moon reflecting the light of the sun, I am trying, clumsily, to reflect the love I feel flowing out of the divine and through the hearts of others.

Chasing after Moonlight

Lifting my eyes to the twinkling sky,
On a cool and a cloudless night,

In spite of the starry beads of silver,
I'm drawn to more mysterious light
Reflecting the fire of a greater flame,
And my stirring soul takes flight.

A small, hardened, and cratered sphere,
Never shining if alone,
But when the sun provides the spark,
It creates a change in tone,
Shadowy trees and glittering streams,
In the familiar, new beauty is shown.

As the moon reflects the burning light
From our system's central pole,
So might I reflect the patient love
Flowing out from the center of the whole:
"You chase after that which enlightens the way."
Be still, my soul.
Be still, my soul.
Be still, my soul,
And pray.

In the love that I reflect and generate, I can make a difference in the world, but my light alone is not enough. Before coming to Uganda, I dreamed with naïve idealism that it might be – that I could save the world from injustice, violence, and needless suffering if I endured in my work. The passage of time has tempered my dreams with humility, showing me that so much of this universe and so many of the difficulties we face are infinitely more complex than they appear to be from afar. While the moon can provide a certain amount of light, it alone provides, at best, only a shadowy, partial view of things. It cannot compare with the light of the sun. The grand, imposing arc of history far exceeds the reach of the minute point that encompasses my relatively brief life.

And yet, there is a dichotomy here. The only place from which a sweeping, historic change can come is one of these points. A single point touches those nearby, and the movement slowly, perhaps sporadically, expands through time and space. Every point has value. Every point can start a turning. Every link, every relationship can lead to growth, development, and new light. With enough mirrors positioned correctly, a dark room can be lit using only the reflected light from the sun.

I'm beginning to approach the end of my two years in Uganda. Time is a funny thing. Sometimes, I feel as if I have been in this place for a lifetime. Other times, as now, I feel that my time here has just begun, even though I can see the two-year mark on the horizon. On the scale of histories, two years is a blink of the eye. For me, living within that flash of time, I feel the ambiguity and the tension between these two seemingly contradictory conceptions. On the one hand, I have experienced and learned so much about myself and my humble place in the world. On the other, it seems that I am only just beginning to understand and perform the work that I am here to do.

A common thought many volunteers express as they are finishing their service and preparing to leave is that now, at the end, they seem to be getting the hang of it. It often takes many months to find one's place in a community, to begin to comprehend the issues facing that community, and to decide – with others in the community – how one or more of those issues might be addressed. Many start to see progress or success as their time is winding down.

In my case, I felt that I began working on projects much sooner – almost at the very beginning of my service – because of the organization where I was placed. However, I still identify with these feelings to a certain extent. After over a year and a half, I feel as if I have finally learned enough to provide intelligent and potentially valuable contributions to our work. I feel comfortable interacting and talking with my coworkers – a feeling that usually takes me a long time to develop, given my introverted personality. Now, nearing the end, I find that there is more to do. I feel as if my work is not done.

Indeed, more time would be valuable for the research I have started for my Master's thesis, and I can do much more to prepare my coworkers at Brick by Brick for my departure, ensuring that they will be able to sustain the work without my contribution. Beyond these practical concerns, though, I realize that I am simply not yet ready to leave. I am considering extending my service for a third year. It will involve getting approval to do so from Peace Corps staff and filling out some paperwork, but I think it would be worthwhile. Certainly, I still experience times when my spirit hits a low point, feeling trapped in a valley. With time, though, these moments seem more like fleeting dips and less like deep, inescapable chasms. A sense of normalcy has settled about this place. It has become a home, and I feel as if I still have more to contribute.

The moon has not made an appearance tonight, but the stars are out. I sometimes prefer these nights, when neither the moon nor the glow of electricity obscures the starlight. When the stars are the only lights in the sky, I can see, in between the brighter ones I recognize, fainter ones that I never noticed before – each one a distant, unquenchable, burning sun. They seem small, but they are so much more than tiny dots of light. Such is our condition. We are small parts of a much grander cosmic reality, and yet the depths of our souls reach within to the center of all existence. Working together, we have the potential to be so much more. Every one of us can make a difference. Is adding on a third year in Uganda the best way for me to make a difference? I don't know for sure, but, as I look to the stars tonight, it feels right.

Look to the Stars

Until we see with truly open eyes,
And we hear with ears that never lie,
And we feel with hands that touch the heart,
We'll never start to recognize our part,
With humble wisdom from the sky.
Look to the stars…

So small and insignificant we seem,
When compared to the lamps that light our dreams,
Diamonds in the universal stream,
And some might say this luminous array
Eclipses even our brightest beams,
But don't fade away…

The girl sitting on the street is all alone,
With downcast eyes, seeing nothing but stone.
Cast out from the life she lived for reasons unknown,
To the cold, where potential seems to freeze to the bone.
So there she waits, thinking it's fate,
Until a stranger comes, hope to create.

Loving and kind, light for the mind,
Her eyes begin to rise, new life to find.

So our worth lies not in well-laid plans,
Nor within our calloused, weary hands,
But inside the heart as it expands.
A tender spark illuminates the dark.
With hope's flame kindled, she starts to stand,
And looks to the stars…

MOVEMENT 7 | SEEING

Songs of Yesterday

Awoken by the slanting beams of light,
As dreams escaping vanished from my sight,
Arising now to walk the forest green,
As squirrels play in sunlight blazing bright
In yonder meadow glazed with dewy sheen,
Detecting something felt but never seen.
This beautiful day, pure and simply done,
I bask in you, for you are in the sun.

Its arc described, that steady, flaming ball
Is sunken, and the evening shadows fall.
In blackened sky appear celestial beads,
Impressed am I, and lullaby recall
From days long past, when newly-planted seeds
Were all I knew of love's suggested deeds.
The memories play, surely nothing bars
My thoughts of you, for you are in the stars.

Galactic eyes, now slowly rendered blind,
Give no more light once layered clouds combined.
Grave voices in the dark I seem to hear,
Groaned workings of a worried, frenzied mind,
But something holds me back before I steer

Completely into chaos lurking near.
I quietly pray, calmly, to embark
On dreams of you, for you are in the dark.

Awoken by the hanging mists at dawn
As blades of sunlight pierce across the lawn.
Along their way, the wetted drops refract
And let pastel, majestic shades be drawn
From nature's fluid palette inexact,
While distant rumbling 'cross the canvas cracked.
An uncertain day holds in misty shrouds
Your varied hue, for you are in the clouds.

The filtered dyes adjust to darker gray
Then suddenly release torrential spray,
Though thunder pounds, I find a peaceful part
Through unforgotten songs of yesterday.
These steady rains recall a beating heart,
Becalmed by beauty and your loving art.
With open eyes, on shifting, stormy ground,
I look for you, and you are all around.

Public transportation remains one of the most irritating parts of life here. Even after two years spent acclimating to the annoyances that come with traveling through the country packed into vehicles too small for the amalgamation of passengers, luggage, and animals inside, I often cannot help allowing these minor nuisances to combine and create a larger sense of frustration and exasperation with the whole process. I find myself in one of these hot and crowded situations right now, as I travel to another volunteer's site in the western part of the country.

It's not all bad, though. Traveling does give me an excuse to spend a large chunk of my day reading, and, when I take a break from the pages of my book, I can look out the window and watch the Ugandan countryside rush by. This morning, a few clouds are in the sky, and the sun brightens the greens and reddish browns that surround the road. Through the various patterns of the day, whether it is the middle of a hot afternoon or the beginning of a cool and shadowy evening, whether the bright blue sky is clear or shrouded by stormy clouds bringing a torrent of water, wind, and lightning, the adjacent panorama of nature is always beautiful to watch.

To me, the topography, at least in the southern and western parts of the country, is similar to that in Pennsylvania. Around Kalisizo and Masaka, rolling hills, often densely vegetated with a diversity of green plant life, characterize the area. Near my family's home in south-central Pennsylvania, a similar landscape is found, although different species of flora and fauna are present, and, in southern Uganda, wide, flat, and winding wetlands cut through the clusters of hills.

Back in Pennsylvania, my family would occasionally take autumn trips up to the northern part of the state. As we traveled north along the Susquehanna River, the surrounding hills gradually grew in size, until we reached the rounded, wooded peaks of the Appalachians, with a variety of colors bursting forth in changing leaves. In Uganda, moving west feels similar. After leaving the rolling, relatively small hills behind, the peaks grow larger and larger, until one reaches the majestic, green mountains of the west. These summits are not always forested and are occasionally dotted with small, jagged rocks. In the Rwenzori Mountains, located on the border between Uganda and the Democratic Republic of the Congo, the tallest peaks are permanently capped with snow.

We are beings with physical and spiritual components. In much the same way as the starry night sky presented a starting point for my spiritual wanderings, I find in the wilderness the beginnings of a path that concerns how our spiritual and moral lives can interact with the physical realm. Watching the diversity of life pass by my window, flowing through the grandeur of it all, nature never ceases to remind me of the wonder, the beauty, and the harmonious functionality that characterize the natural environment.

Slowly, nature has become, to me, the most wonderful cathedral. The sky and its varied splashes of color have become the most beautifully decorated stained glass windows. The forests and streams have become like an altar on which I can offer my humility, reverence, and admiration. Faith is bigger than me and my thoughts. It is bigger than a church or a religion. It encompasses the entire world and every instant within that world. Every experience, every moment can be sacred, if the eyes of the heart are open to see it.

A Stained Glass Sky

Left alone in a quiet cathedral
With wooden columns on either side,
Pacing through a twisting aisle,
Wondering where you hide.

A fluttering greets these expectant ears,
A rush of air blows across this face,
Moves my eyes to locate signs
Of your abiding place.

Consider the glistening walls of green,
Perhaps the floor bearing shades of brown,
Or the old, gray, stone staircase
Draped in a flowing gown.
But then it hits me,
Surrounds, engulfs me
In sudden, revealing rains:
Within it all, your presence, and life
Is coursing through these veins.

Soon light returns
To pierce the storms
And shine on all that's nigh:
Each sacred thing that nature weaves,
Each blade of grass, each blowing breeze,
Each sacred stream, leaf, rock, and tree,
And me,
Beneath a stained glass sky.

While we extol the beauty of nature, though, it's also important to remember that nature is not simply a picturesque backdrop to our lives. Human beings are integrated into the natural system, functioning as pieces that interact, positively, negatively, or indifferently, with other components in that structure. This is true everywhere, but, in Uganda, it is so easy to see how closely we are connected to the land, water, and air around us.

Especially in rural areas of the country, where most of the

population lives, nearly every household is engaged is some form of farming, whether it involves growing local staples like *matooke* or maize, growing cash crops like coffee or tea, or raising animals like pigs, goats, cows, and chickens. In Kalisizo, many people come from the surrounding rural areas to sell their grains, vegetables, fruits, or other products. My three coworkers, Max, Suzan, and Prossy, all contribute to this agricultural productivity. Max and Suzan, who live outside of town, albeit in different directions, grow vegetables and other crops, while Prossy, who lives in town, raises chickens.

It does not end there. Around Lake Victoria, one of the largest lakes in the world, a great number of villages can be found situated along the shoreline. These communities are often economically dependent upon the local fishing industry. Every day, trucks drive out to these settlements on dirt roads to buy the daily catch of the fishermen, who go out on the lake with their long canoes and large nets to make their living, catching mostly tilapia. The fish are transported back to nearby towns or other population centers, where they may be sold directly or are taken to processing facilities. A large processing plant sits just down the road from our office in Kalisizo, and our noses always tell us when the fish trucks drive past.

Tourism is also a large industry in the country, and it relies heavily on the natural world. Uganda contains a number of national parks, where many animals synonymous with life on the African savannah can be found. I've seen lions, elephants, hippos, crocodiles, zebras, chimpanzees, baboons, and even mountain gorillas, which today only live in small areas of a few countries in this part of the continent. In fact, along some of the main roads that run through the southwestern parts of the country, it is possible to spot some of these animals in the nearby fields, or perhaps even on the road itself. I have heard stories of *matatus* colliding with elephants on the road that runs through Queen Elizabeth National Park.

While I am always moved to appreciate the wonder of the natural world when I find myself face to face with these majestic creatures, what I consider to be my favorite natural experience in Uganda took place in a small, relatively little-known park where these iconic African animals do not roam. Between Masaka and Kampala, a narrow dirt road leads away from the beaten path and toward the entrance to Mpanga Forest. This forest is not, like most of the larger parks, surrounded by upscale tourist lodges that offer guests a wide range of amenities. No, just inside the entrance to this park sit three small buildings – a tiny office for a park ranger, a simple, two-bedroom house for guests, and the modest home of the woman who takes care of the guesthouse. The guesthouse does have electricity and indoor plumbing, but, when I visited this place with a friend, the water was not running.

Despite the humble nature of the lodging, which was admittedly still above the level of my house in Kalisizo, the few days spent in this forest may have been the most peaceful and serene that I have experienced in Uganda. Mpanga Forest contains a limited network of trails, where a variety of birds, butterflies, and vegetation can be seen. There is something about walking between the trees, surrounded by the sights, sounds, and smells of life, that draws my soul closer to the heart of all things. While I may not be able to see or describe all of the processes that go on in a diverse habitat like this one, I feel them encircling me. I feel a concentration of relationships in this place, connecting the various organisms and pieces of the earth to one another.

Like us, these natural components also function as points on the surface of the universal sphere. We interact with them, depend on them, and can have a profound effect on them. The world is full of these invisible connections, these threads that bind things together and create vast networks of interdependency. We cannot always see them. They may not be apparent to our senses, but they are there. The things themselves, the points on the sphere, are important, but so are the connections that weave these pieces together. If we do not consider both, we miss the full, interlocking splendor of the cosmos and of this planet. In the forest, in the space between the trees, I can begin to feel these uniting strands and the deep foundations from which they originate.

The Space between the Trees

They say we see the forest but don't see the trees.
They say we climb the branches, not touching the leaves.
They say we see the hive but don't notice the bees,
But we do, yes, we do,
While still we look further and deeper.

Our eyes are not all muddled to see only sky.
Our ears miss not the flutter when birds wheeling fly.
Our lives do not swing shut to each one's tiny cry,
But all through, we search, too,
For threads left unseen by the weaver.

Press fingertips together, calm my beating heart,
Feel active nervous fibers, pull slowly apart.
When fingers stand alone, no sense should make them start,
But they do, yes, it's true,
The cords of connection still quiver.

In space that seems so empty blows echoing breeze,
With remnants of the dreamers who love where it weaves,
So there my spirit fills the space between the trees,
And though you dwell all through,
A lingering breeze makes me shiver.

We are closely connected with the environment around us, and its welfare concerns more than simply keeping a stockpile of natural resources available for our eventual consumption. It is linked with our souls, and local and global ecological health can impact our own physical, emotional, and spiritual wellbeing. And yet, we do not always treat the environment as if it is precious and inherently valuable. Instead, our actions often seem to suggest that we subscribe more to the view of nature as a collection of potential resources for exploitation – as something relegated to serving the demands of economics and capitalism. When did economic power become more central to our thoughts than ecological harmony?

As we endeavor to identify the oppressed or the excluded, listen to their voices, and work together to create a more inclusive and compassionate society, it seems to me that the elements of nature could constitute one of those marginalized groups. In this case, the environment does not have a voice of its own with which to speak, beyond the visible effects of environmental degradation that we might notice if we are looking. Others must speak for it. Others must communicate its worth – its value – which transcends economic concerns.

Today, the world faces a variety of environmental challenges.

Looking at Uganda in particular, some of the most pressing issues are related to overuse of natural resources. A 2010 report from Uganda's National Environment Management Authority described many of these concerns, a few of which include decreasing soil fertility, deforestation, and soil erosion.

With a rapidly growing population highly dependent on subsistence agriculture, soil fertility has been declining for years. Because commercially-available fertilizers are often too expensive for the average farmer, levels of nutrients that are present in the soil diminish over time as those nutrients are mined during each growing season. Once the crops reach the kitchen, they are almost always cooked on stoves and open fires fueled by either firewood or charcoal. The considerable demand for these solid cooking fuels has caused widespread deforestation.

The roots of trees and other vegetation support the structure of the soil and promote the infiltration of rainwater. As forest habitats are destroyed, soil erosion and the possibility of landslides increase. Especially in the eastern part of the country, several major landslides have happened in recent years. Besides the obvious immediate dangers posed by these natural disasters, they also contribute to the already declining soil fertility levels. Some areas of Uganda have reported substantial losses of topsoil and nutrients over the past few years, and, back in 2002, certain soils in the country were already being classified as having low or deficient levels of important nutrients like nitrogen and phosphorus.

Local brick production also contributes to deforestation and has a destructive effect on the wetlands that I see every day snaking through the hills of southern Uganda. Clay-rich soils are needed as the raw material for brick-making, and these types of soils are commonly found in wetlands. As the soil is harvested, wetland area decreases, associated vegetation dies, and many of the benefits that wetlands offer, including natural water filtration and storage, can no longer be provided.

In Lake Victoria, fish populations are waning as a result of overfishing. This trend could have a damaging effect on other life in the lake and on the health of the rivers it feeds. The source of one of the most famous rivers in the world – the Nile – lies here, before the river flows through several countries on its way to the northern edge of the continent. The impacts of each one of these issues extend to touch other organisms, other habitats, and other places, and I can say from personal experience that the mere sight of an environment in the midst of deterioration and decline has a way of polluting the soul, giving rise to feelings of cynicism and futility. The problems that plague the natural world are larger than our individual selves, even though our collective actions or inactions contribute to them, and it is difficult to see how one might go about alleviating their causes and effects.

In the face of these troubles, it may be easy to blame the people who appear to be on the front lines, directly participating in the deeds that cause environmental degradation. In some cases throughout the world, perhaps this assessment of responsibility carries some truth. But, in a place like Uganda, we would be mistaken if we saw people who are simply struggling to find a way to provide for themselves and their families as being more accountable than others. Where fruitful jobs and sustainable livelihoods are difficult to come by, people are easily propelled into exploiting the natural resources that are just outside the door and pushing those resources beyond the limits of ecological equilibrium.

By tacitly taking part in a system that does not adequately value the preservation of nature, forcing those on its bottom rungs to choose between the welfare of the local environment and the wellbeing of their families, we are all collectively responsible. And beyond that, as we allow nature to be harmed, we are also placing future generations of humanity at risk. A lack of respect or concern for the environment we inhabit, or for another creature within that environment, adversely affects everything, including ourselves and what we leave behind for those who will follow.

At the same time, these natural systems provide clues as to how we might adjust or remodel our lives and societies to be more environmentally and socially responsible. I find my mind turning to these topics whenever I walk through a forest, through the spaces between the trees. I look at the trees and see examples we might try to emulate. The branches and leaves of a tree reach for the light of the sky, while their roots delve deep into the soil. Similarly, we all have hopes and aspirations that we reach for, but, without a grounding in reality, history, and humility, we risk being carried off and lost in the gusting winds of adversity.

Shifting to a higher level, in the most resilient, biologically diverse forest ecosystems, individual trees are surrounded by a variety of life – plants, animals, bacteria, fungi, and others. This diversity allows organisms to specialize and cooperate with one another, rather than compete for everything. Competition is relatively inefficient – energy is lost, and large amounts of waste are generated. We see the same, efficient model of specialization and cooperation when we look at the structure of individual organisms. Within a single tree, butterfly, or human being, different pieces perform distinct functions, and they interact, working together in a collective way, for the good of the entire being.

And yet, our economic systems are based on principles of competition and the quest to satisfy individual needs and desires. As such, we might begin to see fundamental issues with these systems. Perhaps most significantly, we might notice the inevitable descent of some to the bottom rungs of the ladder, not necessarily through any fault of their own. We might notice the system's inability to place an accurate value on certain, less quantifiable items, like ethics, compassion, justice, or preservation of the environment. In at least some instances, would systems that place a higher focus on cooperation and the wellbeing of all be more appropriate? Would systems that actively promote a diversity of thought and culture enable us to develop more resilient societies and fuller conceptions of life? Is there a deep wisdom flowing beneath the leaves of the forest that could teach us a better way?

The Life beneath the Leaves

The old oak stood, all knobby and gnarled,
Above the boughs of fledgling brethren.
Defiantly, its knotted strands
Clung fast to life without concession.

The chill wind blew, through branches it snarled.
The old oak's end seemed then to come.
Ostensibly, time's tumbling sands
Composed a final requiem.

The last leaves fell, in spirals they swirled,
To gently touch the hardened ground,

And, stoically, they waited there,
A legacy, to earth still bound.

Now warmer air returns to the world,
And wisdom each young soul receives,
Unknowingly the elder's heir:
The old oak lives in what it leaves.

I like to think the work we do at Brick by Brick might constitute a small step toward a better way. Over the past two years, we have been trying to develop and expand a model in which a construction company, conscious of social and environmental issues, provides employment for local workers and uses its profits to fund projects needed in and identified by the local community. As such, maybe we are working within the current economic system but also suggesting how it might be adjusted to be more mindful of its potential issues and inequalities. I doubt it is a perfect model, and we are only operating at a very small scale. But, so far, it seems to be moderately successful and fruitful, given the contextual realities in this area of Uganda.

Most commonly, the construction company's projects involve building rainwater collection tanks. Especially in southern parts of the country, where annual precipitation is relatively high, collecting rainfall can be a feasible and reliable source of water for households, schools, or other institutions, if water tanks are sized appropriately. Many water projects that occur in developing countries focus on systems that function on a community scale, designed for towns, villages, or other networks of households. They usually incorporate shallow or deep wells with pumps, nearby springs, or surface waters such as lakes and rivers. The systems are often expected to be maintained by local committees that collect fees from users, engage in regular maintenance, and perform repairs when needed. Unfortunately, however, these systems are sometimes not sustained for more than a few years. Their various moving parts often break down and may not be repaired, as a result of poorly functioning committees or an insufficient sense of ownership. Because these systems are often put in place by outside organizations and funding sources, communities may not feel that they are truly responsible for their care and upkeep.

Consequently, there is a slowly growing movement known as "self-supply" that focuses on helping households, most commonly in rural areas, improve their water supplies using their own means. Admittedly, I initially had trouble with this idea. Asking those who already have few resources at their disposal to provide water for themselves seemed a bit questionable. Since water is necessary for health and survival, I see access to safe and clean water as a basic human right, something that should not be determined by one's economic security or access to resources. However, the more I have seen the realities on the ground, the more I have understood that it is an issue of practicality and finding what works. Regardless of who they are for, water systems are pointless if they sit broken or unused.

When people build or buy their own groundwater wells or rainwater tanks, they are much more likely to maintain them and repair them if something breaks. As a household's economic situation slowly improves over time, perhaps due in part to increased access to water, they can incrementally improve the type, capacity, and condition of their water supply. For example, in the case of rainwater collection, they might begin by harvesting water with a few buckets positioned under the edge of the roof. Then, they might add a gutter that drains into a ceramic jar, and, eventually, they might install larger tanks so that the collected supply lasts for a longer period of time.

For this approach to work, local businesses that offer various water supply options – or the materials required for their construction – are needed. If these businesses can operate profitably, the approach can be economically sustainable, something that is difficult to achieve in many types of development work. Brick by Brick's construction company fits into this "self-supply" model, with the relatively large water tanks it builds (5,000 to 30,000 liters) being appropriate for institutions and larger, middle-class households.

Of course, it is not perfect. Systems are not guaranteed to be operated and maintained correctly, and people can still be left out. The households in the worst financial situations may not be able to take advantage of this approach, because they do not have the resources needed to begin the process of investing in their own water supplies. This is where the other side of Brick by Brick's work – the side engaged in community projects – comes into play. Most of these projects occur in nearby public schools, which generally serve the poorer families in the area. We have also partnered with other Peace

Corps Volunteers and their host communities to build rainwater harvesting systems in other parts of the country. These projects are usually supported by small grants funded through the Peace Corps. In all of these undertakings, we work hard to encourage that necessary sense of ownership and to establish the importance of maintenance among the beneficiaries, who are involved in project planning and who make contributions, including certain materials and labor, during construction.

One of these Peace Corps projects is the reason I am now on the road heading toward the western mountains. In the early planning stages, before any construction occurs and even before the application for a Peace Corps grant has been written and submitted, I usually visit the site of a possible project to talk with the volunteer stationed there, the local community, and any institutions or organizations with which we might be working. Seeing the site helps in determining appropriate locations and sizes for the rainwater tanks that would be installed. It also helps us to estimate the materials needed, the overall costs of the project, and a timeline for completion, and to establish, with members of the community, what contributions could be locally provided. For a Peace Corps grant, the beneficiary community is required to contribute at least one quarter of the total project cost, through some combination of purchasing or providing needed materials, equipment, or labor. At the end of one of these site visits, we often have a good idea of what the project will involve, and we have a good start on writing the grant application.

Over the past two years, I've been fortunate enough to work with several volunteers on these types of projects. Admittedly, once we reach the construction phase, the difficulties of working in different parts of the country, far away from Brick by Brick's home area, can lead to issues and misunderstandings. So far, though, these have all been relatively minor, and I think we have been able to move past them to everyone's satisfaction. On the whole, being able to do these projects – to see other parts of the country and interact with other volunteers and their communities to improve access to water – has been one of my favorite parts of our work.

Water is such an important part of us and of the surrounding environment. It makes so much of life possible, and, as with other pieces of the natural world, it can suggest better ways of living our own lives. Take the long roads traversed by raindrops falling in the mountains, winding through forests, percolating through soil, flowing through rivers, and finally coming to rest in expansive oceans as infinitely integrated sections of a greater whole. A drop is engulfed by the ocean, but the entire history and essence of that sea can be perceived within that single drop.

Raindrops in the Mountains

Return, return, oh cloud-born bead,
Condense to fall, and thus be freed.
Cut passage round hard rock and tree,
Return, return, to us, the sea.

As splash ye down 'pon mountainside,
Take time, soak in, with earth abide.
Help flower sprout and branch bear fruit,
Let beauty, life, and love take root,

Until you reach the river's end,
Through falls and turns that downward trend,
When once arrived, combined will be
You with us, and we with thee.

Return, return, oh droplet free,
Return, return, to us, the sea,
And so returned, the path complete,
On wings of light, rise up, repeat.

This is how water travels through diverse and resilient natural ecosystems. It moves slowly, soaking into its surroundings, interacting with the life it finds there, and then gently leaving when its work is done. On the other hand, the more haphazardly we build over top of these areas, the more water speeds through quickly, eroding away parts of the environment and polluting others. Could our lives function in a similar way? Could it be that, when we take the time to look around – to take in and appreciate our environment, to interact with and become part of the life that surrounds us – we contribute to the creation of a stronger society that has greater concern for its most vulnerable segments? Could the hungry forces that push us toward lives of overzealous pace and ever-increasing consumption be gradually eroding and polluting our souls, our relationships, and our capacity for genuine compassion?

Water teaches that life takes time. Development that is sustainable takes time. When a phase of one drop's work is done, the results are gently released, allowed to expand and progress through the influences of others, as the drop continues on its way. Right now, two years into my service, my mind is especially focused on the process of releasing and moving on. My decision to extend for a third year was finalized and approved a couple months ago, but many of those with whom I began this process – many of those in my training group on that first bus ride from Philadelphia to New York – have begun to complete their terms of service. Already, some of these people, who have become important parts of my life for the past two years, are no longer around. Their work with the Peace Corps in Uganda has been released, and they have moved on to other phases of their lives.

Two weeks ago, what is known in the Peace Corps as the Close of Service process began for our group. Every week, a few members of our training group conclude work at their sites, travel to Kampala, fill out the necessary paperwork, go through the required exit interviews and medical exams, and finally, in most cases, head to the airport and leave the country. During the first week, as I watched friends depart while I remained behind, I could not help but feel somewhat melancholy. I found myself retreating into my own mind, becoming less willing to freely interact with those around me. Although I still felt extending my service was the right decision, I suppose the start of this exodus impacted me more profoundly than I had expected it would. Up until this point, I had shared a relatively unique experience with these people, and that support structure was now moving away before my eyes.

By the second week, however, it was becoming obvious that my assessment of the situation had been flawed. First, of course, I could remain connected to those who were leaving, although I have learned that communication across oceans is always more difficult to maintain than communication on a local scale. Even in an age of electronics and globally-accessible networks, physical presence continues to be something special. Secondly, I recently had the opportunity to meet many members of the newer volunteer groups. I discovered, not surprisingly, that these volunteers are also wonderful people, and, while they will not replace completely those from my group who are leaving, they will become a great support structure in their own way. After these meetings, which occurred at a conference outside of Kampala, I returned to Kalisizo, revitalized, rejuvenated, and ready to continue the work I have been doing. I will miss those who are leaving, but I know that, for now, my place remains here.

In about two months, I will be taking a six-week vacation to visit the United States over the winter holidays. This is actually a requirement when a Peace Corps Volunteer extends for a full year. It's probably a good practice. While I have no doubts about my extension, I also feel a strong desire to see family, friends, and the home that I have missed for over two years of service and training. I am looking forward to this upcoming trip, but I am also looking forward to continuing my work here.

Innumerable waves roll through the waters of history. They began as ripples in a silent ocean, far back when the universe began. I wonder if our work might be creating small ripples in the local tides. With more time to interact, to grow, and to love, I wonder if these ripples could expand into something more.

Ripples in the Sea

Smooth, in the darkness, as porcelain glass,
Expansive and silent, no time seems to pass
Until whispered winds of your presence, commencing,
Draw ripples across the still, watery mass,
Traveling outward for leagues before sensing
A faraway shoreline, its dunes crowned with grass.

Watching, when sudden, faint slivers of sun
Exceed the horizon, night's darkness to shun,
To glitter upon rumbling waves in the ocean,
Now white-crested peaks tumbling forward to run,
Spreading across the scarred sand with devotion
To heal all the blemishes time's not undone.

Watching, with feet on the soft, wetted sand,
My toes begin shaping new curves where I stand.

I ask myself what part I've played in the warring
That's harmed our humanity, water, and land.
I, a small pebble, could I be restoring?
The ripples I render your winds may expand...

MOVEMENT 8 | CONSERVING

For Me

"For me," I say, "for me, you see?
The sunbeam's ray, the blooming tree,
The scattered flowers on display,
The starry revelry,
Are all arranged to help me be,
To stay my wont to stray."

"Not so, although we may," you say,
"Begin to know a better way
From feeling living nature's flow,
But universal play
Is not the set of grand ballet,
Mere backdrop for the show."

Transcendent, we, beyond the flow
Someday to see, someday to go,
But nature, too, won't cease to be
Though newborn winds may blow.
The value of her mixed tableau
Is greater than we see.

Returning to Uganda after six weeks of vacation in the United States was, admittedly, a bit difficult. I certainly never doubted that I would step onto the plane last January, but the thought of what I was leaving behind, once again, was prevalent in my mind. During that first flight across the Atlantic Ocean with my Peace Corps training group over two and a half years ago, I was excited and a little anxious about the prospect of living and working somewhere that would be completely new for me. It appeared as a huge change in my life, and most of my thoughts were preoccupied with the approaching unknown. Although I knew that I would miss my family and friends, and perhaps a few comforts and amenities, my mind was focused ahead, on where I was going rather than where I was leaving.

This time around, after having been seasoned by two years of work, I knew this place that was looming ahead of me. During those flights in January, I was thinking about the place I was leaving, the people I wouldn't see and the musical instruments I wouldn't touch for almost a year, and the momentous events that I might miss during my remaining months in Uganda. Being home over the holidays, seeing the people I had been missing for two years, forced me to realize how much I would have enjoyed continuing to be there and seeing those people. For someone like me, who takes a long time to feel comfortable opening up to others – who feels and cares deeply for those people who have become close friends over time, but for whom it is still often a struggle to adequately and tenderly express those feelings – the time away was difficult, more difficult than I had expected.

But, in the face of all these yearnings, I needed, and wanted, to come back. I have also been fortunate enough to find people in Uganda who have become close friends. Beyond that, I have a somewhat vague and indefinable feeling that, currently, my work is here. Let me be cautious, now. I am reluctant to say, as perhaps I once did, that I am supposed to be here, or that my place is only here. I think the universe is much more elaborately structured than that, much too limitless to contain only one best course for each soul. I think the labors of my life can probably be worthwhile and valuable along a number of different possible courses, just as they could be less useful and constructive if still other choices are made and paths are taken. True, my personality, interests, and aptitudes may be better-suited to some courses, rather than others, but I'm not convinced that there is a single perfect course for each of us.

I may be wrong, certainly, but all we can truly know, at least on this side of eternity, is whether the work we do strives to nourish the soul and benefit those around us. As I stand here now in the late afternoon sun, six months later – looking out from one of Masaka's southern hills toward the road that leads to Kalisizo, seeing the stripped slopes that had once been forested, the shrinking wetlands in the valley, the people whose livelihoods depend upon this dwindling environment – I remember why I felt the inexorable impulse to return to this place for a third year. Our work is small and humble, but perhaps it contains the seeds of a transformation. Perhaps it holds the grains of a needed transition toward more sustainable lives – lives where we treat nature as a cherished fellow traveler along the way, and not as the road we trample on to reach our own ends.

In the Light of a Faded Sun

There's a hill upon which, in cool, evening calm,
As the light begins to dim,
I look out on the marsh in the vale ahead,
But a chill, tonight, of foreboding qualm
Strikes me with something grim.

Somehow lessened it seems, that soft, fertile bed,
And the sight from where I stand
Is diminished and darkened by clouds coal-gray,
They repress the flight of the colors spread
Wide over nature's land.

We have mined in the vale for rich, wetland clay,
While the brightly burning wood
Spread a veil o'er the sky as the trees declined.
Are we blind, in spite of what's on display,
Scars that this earth's withstood?

Is it pride that can cloud the air of the mind,
Or can smite our clay-born hearts,
When we take without thinking of others' due,
When we hide the plight of the ones behind,
Yet to receive their parts?

So I pray that we take humility's cue
To contritely live as one
With the earth, as we search for the truth and you
In the light of a faded sun.

It is not pride that pushes the people who depend upon this environment to contribute to its deterioration, to remove more than can be replenished for the children who will follow in our footsteps. Those people who spend their days cutting down trees and digging up wetlands, it is not that they feel some perverse pleasure and sense of power in doing so. Neither is it ignorance that explains their actions. People here are perceptibly and obviously connected to nature, and they can see how it is changing. They don't need a scientist to tell them about environmental degradation or climate change. It is apparent in their lives every day.

Uganda has two rainy seasons over the course of a year. I am told that, in the past, the beginning and end of each season could be predicted almost to the day. Farmers could plan ahead with the knowledge that the weather would adhere to its typical schedule. This may be something of an idealized and simplified description of the past, but I believe that some truth is contained within it. These days, in contrast, much more guesswork seems to be necessary. The rains may start this week, or they might not commence for another ten, fifteen, or twenty days. And the severity and frequency of rainfall during the wet seasons are becoming more variable as well. These factors can mean the difference between a good harvest or a poor one – the difference between a well-fed family with a reasonable income or a hungry one with little or no money to spare for school fees, supplies, or clothing.

The relatively small, individual acts of environmental harm that we see in Uganda every day, compounding as more and more people take part in them, occur because of economic necessity. The bounty of the earth offers us riches that can be exploited, enabling some people with meager or no income to obtain the money they need to survive. I find it incredibly difficult, if not impossible, to blame those who have been forced into these actions. It is so much easier to assign blame to the overarching structures, the huge entities, the callous economic systems that seem to minimize humanity as they seek to maximize profit and that seem to have become ends in themselves. The common focus on money as a primary indicator of quality of life and personal worth can blind us to important parts of life, the parts associated with intrinsic dignity, with responsibility to those around us, with cooperation, and with sharing, rather than with giving and taking.

Undoubtedly, these systems have given rise to much progress, much technological achievement, and much improved standards of living. At their best, they enhance creativity, foster independence and unique personality, and push us to be better than we are. But, these systems can easily drive us toward increased greed, animosity, and self-centeredness, perhaps in part because they feed on something that seems to be a base ingredient of human nature – the desire to accumulate, to harvest as much as possible. Perhaps a system based on competition is the best available option, given the realities of this world. But, in its purest, most unfettered forms, losers and outcasts incvitably emerge, not because they are bad people, but because they are not as adept or well-suited to the rules of the game. Under slightly different circumstances, I could find myself in that situation. It is a thin line of separation. In the end, some of these people may face a choice between exploiting the environment or perishing. Should they be forced to make that decision? Is it anyone's place to judge their actions, springing out of need?

Given the patterns of the past several decades, the elements of nature seem to be losers within the current global system. The emphasis on consumption, accumulation, and exploitation of natural resources has played a significant role in the changes to the climate that are already becoming apparent. Those changes will be felt around the world, but they are expected to affect developing nations most severely. And things like deforestation and wetlands destruction will only make the situation worse. As the world heats up, more energy is in the air, creating new, more variable, and more severe weather patterns. In Uganda and other parts of the world, we are already seeing what appears to be a higher frequency of severe storms, floods, and droughts. Where deforestation has made hillsides bare, powerful rains are much more likely to cause erosion and dangerous landslides. Where wetlands have shrunk, the environment is less able to store and naturally treat the large volumes of water running off nearby slopes, and the rivers, streams, and lakes we depend on for the water we use and drink can become more polluted.

It is not the most hopeful picture, and I realize that I cannot simply stand back and poke blame at the systemic behemoths that appear to be responsible. Fundamentally, these systems have been created, shaped, and sustained by people and their interactions. I have participated – in the choices I've made, in the things I've bought, in the unpleasant images of deterioration and injustice I've pushed away, in my silence regarding these issues. By participating, even superficially, in the systems and structures that have given rise to these economic and environmental wrongs, I have contributed, and on me must lie some of the blame. I am partially accountable.

It must have rained earlier this morning, I suddenly realize. Standing atop this hill in Masaka, I gaze into a pool of water at my feet and find my reflection staring back at me. A single tear falls, carving out ripples in the water. As my reflection wavers, it seems to take on a more sinister and accusing character. I stand above, charged and convicted.

Tears from the Eye of the Storm

Rising winds grow darker, sweep away the sun,
Rumbling din rolls closer, lightning strikes, a second's shade undone,
Swirling hungry masses soon consume the sky,
Surging front so passes, hail's barrage and pounding rains rush by,
While down below, destruction in its wake,
Branches torn from where they grow, as barrows, crumbling, quake.

Crushing floods rise higher, spread across the land,
Felling buttressed spires, overwhelmed, like castles made of sand.
Seemingly more frequent, storms like her now form,
Something somewhat recent, over time, has caused the Earth to warm.
Ascending clime and slowly rising sea,
Here we find conditions prime for stormy energy.

Looking from the center, seeing what she's wrought,
Feeling life resent her, though she knows, her will amounts to naught,
Choosing her own vector proves itself in vain,
Changing winds direct her, pressures shift, releasing falling rain.
So pondering, her painful tears soon pour
Where I stand, now wondering, should we confess to more?

But perhaps, in our complicity and our participation rest the seeds of hope. These systems contain people and the relationships between them. As elements of these systems, we could reorganize and reform into something different – into new ways of living with our environment and one another. Granted, this language is idealistic, perhaps even naïve, and, while I think that our work at Brick by Brick is aimed in this direction, it is certainly not nearly large enough to generate a major global shift toward a different, more environmentally-aware and socially-conscious path. But, at the same time, there is something special about that smallness. I think that the limitations of our scale force us – or perhaps I should say that they allow us – to connect on a more personal level with those we are working with, to develop relationships that span years, and to build up a sense of mutual respect and trust. Only then are we given a truer, more genuine understanding of those around us, the issues within the local community, and the measures that might point toward something better.

Many pieces of our work focus on community and economic development that is also conscious of the environment. The construction company Brick by Brick founded, before I arrived, is wholly based on that principle. The initial idea came about after Jon, the previous Peace Corps Volunteer working in Kalisizo, had learned about Interlocking Stabilized Soil Bricks – or ISSBs – from a professor at Makerere University in Kampala. While the typical, locally-produced burned bricks used for building homes and other structures in the country are made using wetland clay and large amounts of firewood, ISSBs require neither of these elements. By mixing a small amount of cement with water and murram – a subsoil available in many parts of the country – and then by compacting this mixture in a hand-operated press, a team of two of our masons can make about 300 of these ISSBs in one day.

The combination of the cement and the compaction makes them stronger than locally-produced burned bricks, and the ISSBs do not need to be burned after coming out of the press. We just let them sit for about two weeks, giving the cement time to cure. Beyond that, ISSBs are formed so that they interlock with each other, meaning that they fit together nicely when building a wall and that less mortar is needed between bricks, reducing the amount of cement required during construction. We have two presses, one that makes straight

ISSBs and one that produces bricks with a slight curve. These curved ISSBs work well when building cylindrical water tanks, which we do quite a bit. In terms of cost, producing one ISSB costs more than making one burned brick, but it could probably be argued that we're not fully counting the true value of the forests and wetlands being lost as a result of burned brick production. In any case, based on my estimates, the cost of actually building something with ISSBs is comparable to the cost of the same structure built with burned bricks, since we need less cement during construction.

So, if these ISSBs have so many advantages, why are burned bricks much more common? Perhaps most obviously, the ISSB press costs over 1,000 U.S. dollars, which is too expensive for many people, especially when they have limited access to credit. A case could certainly be made that, over time, the initial investment would be recovered, but it remains a difficult hurdle. Indeed, without the help of an investor from the United States, Brick by Brick would have had trouble getting its own ISSB operation started.

Besides that – and besides the fact that some organizations in other parts of the country have had less positive experiences with the technology – inertia can be an extremely strong force. Many people are used to constructing buildings with burned bricks. If a family has the money, burned bricks are the next step above building homes using wooden poles and mud, and an entire supply chain has been created around burned bricks. Loggers cut down trees; the wood is transported to the brick-making operations in the wetland valleys; clay-rich soil is excavated, formed into bricks, and burned; and trucks move the bricks to local construction sites. It's what people are used to seeing and doing, and changing the current system in a significant way would take a long time.

The power of inertia is perhaps nowhere more evident than in the realm of sanitation. Or – as an environmental engineer whose thesis research is focused on this topic – maybe I just think about it more than others. A major focus of my work during this third year of my service has been the introduction of demonstration Ecological Sanitation (Eco-San) systems at two of Brick by Brick's partner schools. The basic idea is this: there is value in what we in the United States usually try to forget about after flushing the toilet. Contained in those materials are nutrients and organic components from the foods we have eaten, and, before that, from the soil where our foods were grown. In places like the United States, large amounts of fertilizer are applied to farmland, providing more than enough of the needed nutrients, and, at the end of the chain, the nutrients end up in the water, where they were never meant to be. High nutrient levels in water bodies have led in many instances to explosions of local algae populations, which can unbalance entire aquatic ecosystems.

If, on the other hand, we were to look to the natural environment as a teacher, we would notice that those nutrients are often returned to the soil. It could be a cyclical flow, rather than a one-directional flow from soil, through crops and people, to water. Eco-San systems are designed with that cyclical principle in mind. They attempt to safely recover the resources that are available in our waste products, so that those resources can be put to use once again, following nature's example.

If the notions of learning from the wisdom of nature and of protecting aquatic ccosystems are not enough, there is also the issue of fertilizer production, which cannot continue as it does today indefinitely. Take phosphorus, one of the most important nutrients contained in fertilizers. There is no substitute for phosphorus, and we need it. It is literally inside our DNA, holding together the codes that allow our bodies to make the proteins they need to function. The phosphorus that is used to produce fertilizer comes from phosphate rock, much of which is mined in a few places around the world. It's unclear how much is left, but, regardless of the specific amount, it is finite. If we continue producing and using fertilizer like we do today, our supply of phosphate rock will run out at some point. One way or another, we need to find ways of reusing the nutrients we already have circulating through our bodies, the crops we eat, and the soils in which they grow.

In Uganda, fertilizer use is not all that common. But, because large amounts of food are still needed, the nutrients that are naturally contained in the soil are being used up without being replenished. Over time, this means that soil fertility declines, along with crop yields. With most people in the country using pit latrines, those nutrients that could be used to replenish the topsoil are ending up deep underground, too deep to be of any help to crops.

So, we have been working to introduce Eco-San systems in cooperation with our partner schools. From others' experiences in various places, we know that these systems are not perfect, nor are they always accepted by local community members. Especially at the beginning, much skepticism surrounds them and the idea of reusing human waste, and, if they are not used correctly, the facilities can become unpleasant. Since these school communities have no experience with Eco-San systems, and since Uganda has little or no tradition of reusing human waste, we have been extremely careful with this project, placing an even greater focus on ensuring local participation and a sense of ownership within the school communities. So far, things have been going well. While students and parents were somewhat skeptical at first, the students are developing a greater appreciation for the system's benefits as they use the facilities, and those students not actually using them are learning from students who are.

As encouraging as these pieces of our work can be, it does not escape me that they are only small drops in an extremely large ocean. I admit, sometimes the issues we face in the world today just feel overwhelming, too big for one person – or even for a group of people – to impact in a meaningful way. Sometimes, despite the hopeful seeds of change I see around me, it feels like the collective inertia of so many factors larger than myself is pushing us, inexorably, further down our current road – a trajectory that could leave so many and so much that is beautiful behind, motionless in its wake.

Waterfell

This place had once been beautiful, a flood of greens and blues.
The breeze had gently cooled the leaves, as birds sang out their news.
Creation called 'cross field and stream, in summer and in snow.
Life was drawn from far and wide, by the rumbling down below.

Where has the tide of life been turned? What caused this place to lose
Its singing birds, its rustling leaves, its lush and soothing hues?
The rumbling down below has ceased, since diverted was the flow.
Creation forsaken, too much was taken, and the level fell too low.

Remember the tale of this barren cliff, only the wind remains to tell,
Screaming through dry, bare, broken branches, in a place called Waterfell.

My occasional trips to Kampala can sometimes have this effect on me. I don't go to the city willingly. Every trip is predicated on the need to attend a meeting or to take care of something at the Peace Corps office. I've never been a city person, preferring the relative calm and quiet of the country. The center of Kampala is a crowded, commercial, concrete jungle that I could do without. But, I certainly can't deny that the world is becoming more urbanized. More than half of the global population now lives in urban areas, and the number is only expected to continue rising. In some ways, cities can function more efficiently than rural settings, because resources can be consolidated and concentrated in one location, rather than needing to spread out across widely dispersed areas. But, for me, this environment of right angles, of gray and glossy geometry, of manufactured sound and light – in contrast with the smooth undulations and spontaneous symphonies of the natural world – provides a stark reminder of how much humanity has impacted the planet on which we live.

One of the most striking things about Kampala is the traffic. "Oh, the jam," Max calls it. Regardless of the time of day, the streets are filled with a plethora of cars, *matatus*, and *bodas*, swerving and snaking through openings hardly larger than themselves. Honking car horns, accelerating engines, and the voices of *matatu* drivers calling out their routes to potential passengers fill one's ears. This glut of sound and activity finds its hub at the city's main taxi park, where vehicles slowly maneuver like pieces in a sliding puzzle, and where the sidewalks are always filled with a sea of humanity.

Kampala is built on a series of hills, with this central taxi park being somewhere close to the bottom of all of them. Gravity seems to draw everything in this direction, including the pollution of thousands upon thousands. Besides the lingering fumes expelled into the air by the multitude of automotive engines, there is a wide drainage channel that runs along one side of the newest portion of the taxi park, filled with the refuse of so many shop vendors, travelers, and drivers. Looking at the water in this ditch, which, most likely, eventually flows into Lake Victoria, it is easy to see how we can seriously impact the environment around us – how we are harming the natural world on which we depend.

Perhaps even more apparent than the environmental issues are the economic ones. As with any city, I suppose, its different sections reveal inequalities between its residents. Atop Kampala's several hills are communities with something of a suburban flavor, containing the large, guarded, walled-in compounds of upper-class residents. Foreign diplomats, as well as staff members of some NGOs and international development agencies, also live in these areas. In stark contrast are the slums and the crowded groups of homes located at lower elevations and on some of the hillsides. Around the outskirts of the city, where low-lying wetlands surround the hills, unplanned settlements are expanding, further damaging those crucial wetland ecosystems and providing people with a relatively unstable foundation for their homes.

Back near the center of the city, walking its streets, one passes beggars of a variety of ages and with a range of evident health conditions. It is most difficult to see the young children, some barely old enough to walk, sitting on the concrete, eyes half-closed, somewhere between uneasy sleep and stifling reality, hands frozen in front of their bodies, palms upward, in a perpetual appeal. Despite appearances, I am told that many of these children are not on their own, that someone behind the scenes is placing them on the streets, and that any money the children have at the end of the day is seized by this person in the shadows, deviously playing on the genuine compassion and charity of others for innocent children. As with so much of development work, what seem to be acts of simple charity quickly become more complex, can have unintended consequences, and do not address the root causes of the problems we see.

It is true, these various issues can, and do, plague less highly-populated areas. But cities – especially when the less attractive parts are not effectively hidden away – concentrate those issues, allowing us to more clearly see the effects of our lives on at least some of the outcasts, the marginalized, and the oppressed. They show us that a better way is urgently needed, that we must quickly learn to live in greater harmony with one another and with our surroundings.

Trees of Glass

Trees of glass on concrete grass,
Past cliffs of brick and mortar,
Metal leaves and canopies,
With wiry veins of copper,

Vines of steel, entwined reveal
The urban forest's border,
Black-paved streams form hardened seams
From one part to another.

And everywhere electric stars
Pacify the night,
Fluorescent or incandescent jars
That flood the dark with light.

Needed, this center of production? Perhaps,
But let not one forget:
The engines of time can make memory lapse
If nature goes unmet.

Look! Out there
Beyond the lighted square,
Past where the pavements end,
Are other worlds of life to share,
To care for, and to mend.

Once, you see,
Before our lives could be,
The world out there was here.
True grass and leafy canopy
Lived under stars so clear.

But then that life was stolen
To make way for us and progress,
While we gave back unnatural poison
And called it nature's conquest.

The thing we now must all remember:
Our life begins out there,
With trees and streams and sunlight's ember,
Connections pure we share.

So trees of glass with nature's grass,
The former with the latter,

Must learn to live in harmony,
Or else, all will shatter.

What is this better way? What could lead to the healing of the world around us, of our relationships, and of ourselves? I can't say that I know for sure, but I am becoming more and more convinced that it has something to do with love, something to do with the force that builds, brings together, and renews life. It has something to do with a wholesale change in heart, a change that leads us to see the shared nature of our lives – to see ourselves reflected in those who appear to be different from us. With some small changes in my own life, I could have been someone on the outside looking in. Perhaps, in some ways, I am, without even knowing it.

It comes from within ourselves, but it also transcends us. At the same time as I acknowledge others' similarities with me, I also need to recognize the differences, the unique attributes of each person I encounter. While it can be easy to accentuate the distinctions between different groups, it is also all too simple to paint everyone with one, unchanging brush. We are not totally separate, and we are not completely uniform, as if we were identical bricks in a wall. This dichotomy – that we are collectively linked and individually unique – can only be completely realized through open, loving, compassionate relationships with one another. And then, within that foundational structure, we can work together for good.

This, to me, is at the core of effective development work – building relationships across cultures and social boundaries. It is a slow process, a longer road to walk – longer than coming in, doing a tangible, concrete project, and leaving – but I think it's worth it. I've heard too many stories of those quick, in-and-out projects failing after a year or two. I've seen too many broken water pumps and crumbling, empty storage tanks. Of course, these pieces of infrastructure are important, but, without long-term, personal connections, they are often not sustained.

As my service is nearly over, people have started asking those questions that often come at the end of significant life experiences. "What was the best part? What was the best thing you did?" I find myself thinking back over the projects we have done, the many water tanks we've built in several communities across the country, and I realize that, despite the importance of these systems for people's wellbeing, they are not what I find to be most significant. For me, the most significant pieces are the relationships, the interactions with the people I've worked closely with over the past few years – seeing their progress, feeling comfortable with them, and knowing that I have a place in their hearts, just as they have a place in mine.

Not too long ago, I spent Easter weekend – that time so focused on the renewal of life – with Max, Teddy, and their children. As Easter Sunday drew to a close, after the huge meals, after the movies watched on the small television set, after the time spent reading on the couch, and after others had gone to bed, Max and I were sitting alone in the living room.

"Thank you, John," Max said as we started to stand up.

"Well, I didn't really do anything," I replied, thinking of all the work Teddy put into our meals.

"Thank you for spending Easter with us."

"Well, thank you for inviting me to spend it with your family."

"Oh, we could never forget you," Max said, "You are part of the family. We are just praying that God will keep us close in the future."

It took a long time to reach this point, but the process was simply a collection of connected moments – moments in which we chose to work together rather than apart, in which we put our disagreements and differences aside to focus on something greater. Every instant is a new beginning. Every relationship can grow the love in the world. Every life can be the start of a change that will echo across the years. In a single moment, the history of everything converges into one reality, and the possible futures branching out from that point are infinite. We are small, but, in the connections we make, in the actions we take, we can help to choose a road of greater love, greater justice, greater peace, and greater hope for a better world.

The Branches of Time

Streams on shallow slopes converge,
Fed by falling rains,
But then at river's end diverge
To distend in delta's veins,
Depositing their pregnant loads
On branching liquid roads.

Roots in fertile soil submerge,
Nourishment is drunk
To help the branching poles emerge
From the sturdy central trunk,
And leaves caress the silken sky,
With blossoms blooming nigh.

Both in water and in wood,
Twin examples shown
Of how each passing moment could
Lead to better paths unknown,
If we would see what has been sown
Where winds of time have blown.

Histories have coalesced
And have brought you here
To this one moment. Choose the best
Branch on which to bring us near
The place where life will ever thrive
And leaves of peace appear.

MOVEMENT 9 | LEAVING

Parting Words

This song has been sung,
The gong has been rung,
Now let it resound in years hence,
Composing with ear
To those I leave here,
Who new verses now will commence.

It is November of 2014, and, after a bit more than three years in Uganda, the end is here. Two days ago, I was at the Peace Corps office in Kampala, finishing up my final medical exams, paperwork, and exit interviews. At the end of the day, I rang the gong that hangs just outside of the office's main entrance, a tradition signaling that my Peace Corps service was complete.

I have mixed feelings, but I do feel like it's time to move on. I have learned much about myself over the past three years – about my faults and weaknesses, about my interests and hopes, and perhaps a bit about my place. I have discovered that the best place for me may not be on the ground, implementing development projects.

Before coming to Uganda, I was pretty convinced that it was. I certainly enjoy this work, and being able to work closely with the people around me has been one of the highlights of my service. However, more and more, I have realized that my personality may not be ideally suited for this context. I am introverted and inward-looking, I am not a good conversationalist, I do not like to be the center of attention, and I prefer to let someone else do the talking. Now, in many situations, ensuring that my Ugandan colleagues took on a project's central leadership roles was a good thing. But, occasionally, these traits of mine resulted in interactions that were less successful than they could have been. Undoubtedly, there was – and still is – plenty of room for improvement, improvement that might have made me a better volunteer. But, at this point, I think I also need to accept that, to some extent, these personality traits make me who I am. Realistically, changing them may be unlikely, and I'm content to leave at least some of these traits as they are.

Similarly, looking specifically at my work with the construction company, I don't see myself as the most appropriate person to lead this type of effort. I certainly understand the importance of construction. Without it, no infrastructure projects can possibly reach a conclusion. A set of calculations or drawings remains simply that – an abstraction laid out on a piece of paper. Construction is needed to make it tangible and to ensure that it benefits people. However, even though I have learned a great deal about construction techniques, planning, and management during my time here, I still have little experience and practical knowledge, both of which are extremely important in this field. I can study everything ever written about brick-laying, but, without actually picking up a trowel, I can't completely understand what happens during the construction process. I definitely enjoyed spending time with our masons, but I didn't do their work. My attempt to do so would have been inferior, causing them to lose time and efficiency as they went back to correct it. I understand the fulfillment that can come from building something, but I don't have the experience to be truly effective as a construction engineer. Perhaps most importantly, I've found I am more interested in other aspects of the overall process.

All of these factors have led to the realization that it is time to move on. In January, I will be returning to the University of South Florida for a final semester, as I finish writing a thesis focused on the Eco-San systems we introduced at two local schools. I have found this work, which is more research-oriented but still directly applicable to environmental issues and development work, to be of great interest for me. After that, I'm not sure yet, but I've started looking into the possibility of staying in school for a doctorate, doing research along similar lines.

At the same time, though, moving on is a hard thing. Honestly, sometimes I wonder if part of the reason I extended my service was because it was the safe option, the option that didn't force me to start thinking and making decisions about the next phase of my life. Of course, I had other reasons, but I can't deny that remaining in Uganda – living in the same community, working with the same organization – allowed me to postpone the looming transition.

As good and necessary as change can be, it's also a hassle. It's a lot of work, even though it can be exciting, once I overcome the initial resistance of my own inertia. It has just been so much easier to focus on where I've been and what I've been doing here, than to think too deeply about what might happen next. Three years may not seem like an incredibly long span of time, but, from my current perspective, much of what I did before coming to Uganda feels like a distant memory. This life, here in this place, has become the norm. If, in my mind, I picture myself working, I see myself in our small office in Kalisizo, sitting at the desk where I've sat for the past three years, occasionally looking up to gaze out of our open door at the cows grazing in the football field. If I picture myself cooking, I find myself slicing vegetables on the little table in my front room, next to the propane stove. If I picture myself sleeping, it's in my back room, beneath my green mosquito net, on a mattress that dips in the middle after years of use.

When I think about my life, I am thinking about places, events, and people in Uganda. This is not to say I have not often thought of my friends and family in the United States. I have, and the fact that I will soon be closer to them is certainly a positive aspect of the impending change. Maybe I've simply come to realize that part of my heart lives in Uganda and will, perhaps, always remain here.

Is this, I wonder, part of what sets a long-term overseas position apart from a short-term trip? As annoyed as Peace Corps Volunteers can get when we see short-term volunteers who think they understand everything, I can't deny that short-term experiences have value. Those types of trips introduced me to a broader world and are what began the thought process that eventually led me toward Peace Corps service. Now that I have experienced both, though, it's easy to see the differences. Short-term trips can be very fulfilling and eye-opening, but, regardless of how much experience is packed into those few days or weeks, one will barely skim the surface. Only certain aspects of the situation will be seen, and a person can easily come away from the experience with an idealized or mistaken impression. It is easy to see seemingly simple solutions to problems when the complexity of the context is not completely grasped.

A longer stay can provide a richer, and perhaps a more realistic, experience. I certainly don't claim to have a complete understanding, or a totally accurate view, of Uganda. I've seen things almost every day that I don't think I'll ever understand, and I'm sure that some parts of life here have escaped my vision. But, to a certain extent, I think that I have been able to see some of the various and complex realities of this place. I can see its strengths and weaknesses, its benefits as well as its blemishes. And, despite the difficulties and frustrations that I have seen and experienced over the past three years, Uganda has found its way into my soul. It has had an impact on me, one that I think is for the better.

I'm forced to wonder, though, about my own impact on this place. I hope that the work I've done here has had a beneficial effect, even if it is only a very small one. Has it? I know that we have completed a number of projects. We've built over fifty water tanks across the country, along with several other structures at our partner schools. I've helped Brick by Brick to modestly expand its operations – all accomplished with the crucial contributions of my coworkers, of course. But still, I ponder. Beyond those physical achievements, have I lived by the lessons I've learned? Have I identified the oppressed and marginalized, and have I shown them love and acceptance? Have I stood with them against hatred, injustice, and indifference? Or have I let these things go undone?

What Do You See

What do you see when looking at me?
Does the sight reveal me to be someone who's fought
For the dignity stolen from outcasts forgot,
Or does it illuminate some tendency
To stand aside, free, while others are not?

What do you hear when following me?
Does the sound linger on from a voice wholly spent

121

In support of the voiceless with just discontent,
Or does empty silence suggest, tacitly,
Injustice is that with which I assent?

What do you feel when thinking of me?
Does the sun of your soul start to shine when it sees
My unyielding defiance of hate's crushing breeze,
Or does the warmth freeze as I cower and flee
Or, passive, observe this spreading disease?

What do you see? The truth, if you please…

Honestly, I don't know. I can vividly remember some instances when I was more insensitive, less loving, and colder than I could have been and probably should have been. To be fair, in some of these situations, my irritation was perhaps understandably provoked by others around me. I find myself reminded of something that happened very early in my service, something that I can look back on with laughter now, but that did not seem so amusing at the time.

During the first few months in my compound, it was often very quiet. Before other families moved in, it was just me and my landlady's family. One afternoon, her young son, Ligani, and I were the only two people around, and he was still in the habit of calling me *mzungu*. As I went outside, crossing the compound to use my latrine, I could feel his gaze following me, and, once I had reached the small structure and gone inside, I heard him shuffle over until he was in front of the door. He started playing with the outside latch, moving it back and forth. Through the door, as calmly as I could, I told him to stop. Eventually, he did, probably more a result of boredom than of my appeals. He walked away and left the compound completely. After a few minutes, I pushed on the door to leave. It didn't open. He had left the latch locked. He had locked me inside a latrine with barely enough room to turn around, and no one else was nearby.

Fortunately, I soon noticed that the walls of the stall didn't quite extend the whole way up to the roof. I saw a little space, maybe one and a half feet high, between the top of the wall and the higher part of the sloping roof. Pulling myself up to look over into the adjacent stall, I could see daylight. The door was hanging open. If I could just climb this plastered, six-foot brick wall, squeeze myself beneath the roof, and lower myself down on the other side, I would be free.

Hoisting myself up, I engaged in some minor contortions to get my right leg over to the other side. At this point, I was straddling the wall, with my upper body pressed against the top layer of bricks so that my head could squeeze under the lower part of the roof. After a moment of rest, I slid my left leg over and gingerly lowered myself down on the side of freedom, ensuring that both feet landed on the floor and not in the hole.

Stepping forward through the door, I breathed the free air once more. With enough illumination to see things in detail, I soon realized how dirty my clothes and hands had become. Before I spent too much time dusting myself off, however, I experimented with the lock on my latrine door until I figured out how to position it perfectly, making it impossible for this same situation to occur a second time. Luckily for Ligani, I couldn't find him that afternoon, and perhaps that was a good thing. My prevailing mood was not one of patience and understanding.

Despite that inauspicious beginning, as well as several bumps along the way, my relationships with Ligani and the other children who populate my compound have come a long way. Now, I can truly look back on that unpleasant experience and find the humor in it. However, this progression has not precluded other events from trying my patience.

Based on my appearance, the impression that many people immediately form is that I have only been here for a short time, that I don't understand any of this place's common practices, and that I have a lot of money. Thankfully, having actually lived here for a span of years, many residents of the Kalisizo area no longer make these assumptions. At least, that seems to be the case. When I travel to other parts of the country, however, these issues are more prevalent. Being seen in that way, as a gullible and oblivious rich person, wears on me after a while. The longer it goes on, the more my frustration builds, before eventually bubbling over.

Although, if I am able to take a step back and think about it objectively, can I blame people for seeing me in this way? For better or worse – and perhaps some of both – this country often feels as if it has been overrun with international NGOs, and with the foreign employees and volunteers who accompany them. Ugandans have become accustomed to seeing projects go up and funds given out, on a large scale and on a small scale. The appropriateness and long-term wisdom of some of these activities can easily be called into question, but strong incentives, usually tied to donor funding, can push organizations to get in and out quickly, to build or distribute as many units as possible, and to do so without ample consideration for the contextual suitability of these actions. And so, some Ugandans may look at someone like me and presume that I have limited local understanding, but large pockets of money. Can I blame people for having this idea?

Even if I try to maintain this somewhat more objective and understanding viewpoint, however, it does not shield me from frustration. Just a few weeks ago, I was in Masaka with my coworkers, and we were getting ready to head back to Kalisizo. As I was slowly walking, slightly behind the rest, a man came up to me and began talking, mostly about a local school. It didn't take long for me to realize that he was hoping I could provide some assistance for him and this school. I told him that I couldn't provide the money he was hoping for. After hearing this, instead of letting it go, he asked me if I could go with him to the school anyway. "You see," he explained, "if I bring you and show you to them, then they will think I am making progress."

In the past three years, I have experienced a wide array of odd and uncomfortable situations – being given special service at a restaurant, being placed in a seat at the head table during a graduation ceremony, noticing young men in the Kampala taxi park walking behind me and trying to unzip my backpack, watching children on the street walk up to me and openly reach into my pockets. Some, like this recent experience concerning the man and his school, are extremely awkward and unpleasant. Others are less so, but all serve to call attention to me, to accentuate the apparent differences between me and those around me.

In total, they have sometimes created an environment in which I have found myself becoming less considerate and more callous. I'm not trying to justify it or to pass off blame. I'm simply trying to suggest how it might happen to someone, gradually, over time. I once thought myself to be awfully patient and kind. After being tested, I have found myself to be less so. All I can do is humbly acknowledge my weakness and try to do better.

And yet, I am not leaving with a bad taste lingering in my mouth.

Rather, looking back on everything, I feel pretty good about the past few years. I know that I did not always act as I should have in every circumstance. I know that I did not change the entire country for the better. But, in my little corner of it, I did something, small as it was. I'm not thinking of the water tanks we built or the classrooms we renovated, the fuel-efficient stoves we installed or the Eco-San toilets we promoted. As important as all of these things are for the health and wellbeing of their owners and the surrounding communities, they are not what I consider to be my personal impact on this place.

None of those things would have been possible without a vast assortment of people, from the teachers at our partner schools to our masons, from the directors of our organization to the other volunteers who worked with us, from the neighbors who accepted me to the children who brightened my day. Most importantly, Max, Prossy, and Suzan made it all happen. It is my connection to them, the days spent together working, persevering through difficulties and complications – the serious discussions we had, the joyful laughter we shared – this is what I see, over and above anything else. My relationships with them define my impact.

They may seem like such small things, these relationships, but I was recently shown how significant they can be to the people affected by them. Last week, my coworkers organized a going-away party for me. All of the masons came, and several nearby volunteers also made their way to Kalisizo. Brick by Brick's director, Marc, was there, and so was David, a young Ugandan man who recently graduated from an engineering program. He has been working with Brick by Brick for the past few weeks, and I have been doing my best to train him so that he can continue many of the tasks that have been my responsibility for the past few years. I think, and I hope, he will do well.

At the party, as we were finishing dinner, several people got up and talked about the impact I've had on them. I think I saw Marc, the organization's director, started to tear up a bit as he was talking about my service. Suzan was so appreciative as she described some of the skills I had tried to help her learn. Prossy surprised me with some of her own poetry and later told me that my mixture of hard work and thoughtfulness had pushed her to spend some time on her own creative pursuits. And Max – well, I think I'll come back to him a bit later.

I've found my feelings about this experience to be somewhat difficult to describe. I was overwhelmed and humbled, to be sure. It's a rare and precious thing when so many friends describe, over the course of a few short minutes, just how much I've meant to them. I tried to express my appreciation and to explain how important they have all been to me, but I doubt that my words fully communicated my feelings. I don't know if they could have.

After I walked home, the events of that night continued to ring in my head. I had the privilege to hear and see the impact I was leaving in this place. But it was not the only thing that would remain behind.

What is Left

What is left to say today
After all's been said,
Once we dine and dance and pray,
Then adjourn to bed,
Where the voices fade away,
Echoes in my head?

Friends, like family so dear,
Sat surrounding me,
Some from far and some from near,
Drops of one same sea.
Heartfelt gifts you've shown me here
Given lovingly.

What is left to light the night
After full moon parts?
Embers burning ever bright,
Kindled by your hearts,
Shining from the mountain height
Where your kindness starts.

So each goes a separate way,
With exception slight:
Pieces of my heart did stay
With you upon this night.

Yes, I have been fortunate to meet some wonderful friends here. This simple fact may be the most difficult part of leaving. My coworkers, my neighbors, and of course the other volunteers in the area – all important parts of my life, all beautiful people in their own right. The cliché is that other volunteers are the only people who will every truly understand this experience. In many ways, there is truth in that statement. Who else can fully empathize with my distaste for public transportation, my annoyance with the constant cries of *mzungu*, or the sense of satisfaction felt after making what may appear to be very small and incremental progress?

This afternoon, before using public transportation for the final time to reach the airport in Entebbe, I spent a few hours in Masaka with many of these volunteers. After ringing the gong at the Peace Corps office two days ago, I traveled back to Kalisizo yesterday, to clean out the rest of my house, giving many things to my neighbors and coworkers in the process, and to grab the small amount of luggage I would be bringing back to the United States. Fortunately, this trip gave me one final chance to spend some time saying goodbye to these friends, none of whom were here at the beginning. After most of my own group had gone, I found in these newer volunteers a wonderfully fun group of friends, and they helped me, more than they know, as I navigated my third year.

Now, sitting in Entebbe's small, hot airport, waiting for the late-night flight that would take me away, I look back on my time here with fondness. I know, by holding my friends close to my heart, by remembering how I feel when I'm around them, I will carry a part of them with me. I'm thankful for these connections of the soul that allow our love and care to stretch across time and space.

I begin to look forward to those I will see very soon. I think of those connections that, of late, have most often touched my heart. Over the past couple months, my thoughts have often lingered on my grandmother. She had gone into the hospital for surgery, and, during the procedure, she suffered a stroke. In the days immediately following this incident, her condition was uncertain, but she slowly began to recover. She is now living with my parents, who are taking care of her. From what I have heard, she is continuing to make progress, but it will be a long process.

During those initial days, I found myself feeling somewhat helpless, knowing that medically I could do nothing, but still wishing

I could be there. Every morning, I would open up my computer and anxiously check email, expecting another update from Mom. It didn't take long for me to turn to poetry. It provided me with a place where I could direct the emotions that were beginning to spill out, made all the more intense by the closeness of my leaving and the thoughts associated with that.

Putting pen to paper, I found myself reflecting on Grandma's life. Of course, I had only seen a portion of it, but, from what I did know, I was struck by her quiet, unassuming grace, her soft yet constant love. Hers is a life that slowly reveals its working over many years, gradually unveiling its effect, an effect that is seen most clearly in the devoted relationships of family and friends, and in the values of compassion and kindness that characterize those connections. In her life, I see a gentle spring of love that touches the parched sand around it, slowly quenching its thirst and filling it with life.

A Spring in the Desert Sand

No travelers roamed the barren waste
That lay between these yellow dunes.
No season's break brought wet monsoons
To quench the dry tongue parched of taste.
But now the strands of life are laced
Through what was once a lifeless land,
For here, reflecting patient moons,
Is a spring in the desert sand.

Miraculous, it has appeared,
Has risen from the ground below.
Its streams spread wide to wander slow
And by surrounding heights be steered.
So through the years, it is endeared
To each hard place where trace be found
Of life that now takes root to grow,
Where the water has softly wound.

Decades pass, a green oasis
Lies now between the yellow dunes,
Though still no season's wet monsoons

Form this living island's basis.
Gentle spring took barren stasis,
Transformed it into fertile land
Through patient love o'er many moons,
You're my spring in the desert sand.

As I consider her life, I think of my own. I think of my time in Uganda and the impact it might have. I wonder if it could follow a similar progression. I have made a small difference in the lives of a few, and they have made a difference in mine. These relationships themselves are not world-changing, but they could act as a seed, slowly growing into something more. They could, over time, demonstrate the greatness of smallness – that developing seemingly small relationships, especially ones that cross borders and boundaries, is at the core of creating a better world.

As I consider her healing, I think of my own. I recall the words of my tumble down the waterfall, as the flight that brought me here more than three years ago took off. I remember, as the water enters and reveals us, in the knowing of our flaws it heals us. Among other things, this place has revealed to me the intricate beauty of the world, the complex nature of the people in it, and the shortcomings and blemishes within my own life. By allowing this experience to affect how I live, to change my way of looking at life, perhaps I can work toward my own healing. By holding it close as I go peacefully into the night, perhaps I can be an active participant in the global healing of our relationships with one another and with the world around us.

My flight is beginning to board. I suppose it's time to go. What else is there to say? It's close to impossible to encapsulate three years of life in some sort of final statement. It makes me think of the little cakes that are sold in shops all over this country – break off a section, and the whole thing might start to crumble. Every piece of my time here has been important and has shaped the whole, and the overall experience would be less without any single piece, regardless of whether that piece is good or bad. I'd like to think that we've done some good, and I'd like to think that I've begun to learn from the bad. At the moment, I might have some ideas and hopes about the effects of my time here, but I can't fully know. What will show those effects, over time, are the ways in which I and the people I've encountered use the experiences of the past few years to move forward.

As I step forward through the gate, my mind can't help but return to the one man who has been with me through it all, from the day I began my service all the way to yesterday evening. My trip back to Kalisizo had one other purpose, which I haven't yet mentioned. Late in the afternoon, I met Max at Brick by Brick's office, and he took me out for what he called our "Last Supper". There had been the group dinner a week before, but I'm glad we had the chance to spend this final evening together, just the two of us. As we talked over our food, as Max told me about his children's recent progress in school, about Teddy's activities in their village, and about the young, orphaned boy they had recently adopted, I realized, even more than before, just how much he has meant to me. He was there at the beginning, and he will continue to be there after I've gone.

Admittedly, I had little work experience before coming to this country, but I can say with certainty that I have never had a closer, more comfortable working relationship with anyone in my life. Yes, we've had our disagreements, but I think we've always been able to work through them relatively easily. Max has been my adopted Ugandan father over the past three years, and I feel so fortunate to have developed a genuine, honest, and caring friendship with him. It is within people like Max, as well as Prossy, Suzan, and the others with whom I've worked, that hope for the future of Uganda truly lies. I thank Max for his dedication, his humor, and his support. My life here would have been completely different without him. I hope that moving forward with the next phases of my life will, at some point, lead me back to him, and to this place, once again.

Following the Setting Sun

The shadows lengthening, the stars awakening,
As the light starts to fall,
With twilight beckoning, a time of reckoning
That I might want to stall
Is growing closer as the moon ascends the sky,
And gold and silver light a sweet and sad goodbye,
For after this day is done,
I'll be following the setting sun.

It seems so long ago, when sunlight's morning glow
Gently played in the wood,
A few first steps revealed, but all the rest concealed
In the shade where you stood,
I walked and I learned with each step along the way,
It twisted and turned, with your help I'm here today,
But now that this road is run,
I'll be following the setting sun.

One moment more
Looking back at what came before,
Now I can't be sure
What the future might hold in store.

The final rays invite, then fall away from sight,
And I'm shown it is time,
It may be frightening, yet we have light to bring,
As unknown paths we'll climb,
This day is over, but its lessons will linger on,
And you will never leave my heart after I have gone,
Continue what we've begun
While I'm following the setting sun.

MOVEMENT 10 | LEARNING

The Next Step

I've heard the first step is the hardest,
But sometimes I don't agree.
I've heard the first step is the largest,
But sometimes it seems to me
The first step is something new, exciting,
Or maybe for others to see,
And though, against momentum it's fighting,
It strays not too far from the tree.
With each one after, as long as we're thinking
(And that is a crucial key),
Comes a choice to press on, recommitting, not shrinking:
The next step, still harder, will be.

As I flew out of the country on that warm November night, I began to look forward to the next few steps of my life. Fortunately for me, my status as a Master's International student gave me a degree of certainty as I moved on. I knew that I would begin by spending time with my family, and I would then need to go to work in Florida, finishing my thesis. After that, my plans were less certain, but some ideas and possibilities were beginning to take shape as I crossed the Atlantic Ocean and returned to the United States.

After landing in Washington, D.C., the rest of the year was spent at my parents' house in Pennsylvania, requiring me to brave the beginning of a cold winter. I had grown unaccustomed to these frigid temperatures during my time in Kalisizo, less than a single degree south of the equator. Despite the chill (alleviated to some extent by the house's wood stove), there is a warmth in that Pennsylvania home that is not connected to climate. It still feels like the home I can always return to – my most fundamental home – even now that I have come to think of other places as home as well. As much as I appreciate that I could feel at home in Uganda, and as much as I hope that I can feel at home wherever my future life takes me, there's something special, something irreplaceable, about being in that house, with those people, where so much love, warmth, and care exist.

This six-week stay in Pennsylvania allowed me to spend the holidays with my immediate and extended family, to see Grandma every day, and to reconnect with friends whom I had often thought of, but had seldom talked to, over the past few years. I slept in the room where I had grown up, once more reminded of my good fortune. To be surrounded by those who love me, to feel the immediacy and potency of their care and concern for my well-being, and to know they will support me through anything – these are just a few of the benefits of a devoted family. I've felt these things before, but, as is now the case with so many aspects of my life, they have become colored, informed, and transfigured by my experiences across the sea.

Late one evening, about halfway through my time in Uganda, I heard a knock on my door. It was one of the women who helps to run a nearby guest house. She had been sent to invite me to a graduation party for my landlady's daughter, Maria, and the party was beginning at that moment. After quickly changing into something a bit more presentable, I made my way to the guest house, less than a minute's walk away. In those few seconds, I took in the beautiful night. The stars were out, and the yellowish moon, just past full, was shining brightly down onto the guest house's courtyard. Knowing that I would probably become the center of attention as soon as I appeared, I paused and took a breath at the entrance.

As I approached the group, chairs and tables quickly parted to provide me with a place to sit. In his haste, one man grabbed the top of a small table, not recognizing that the legs were unattached, and, without realizing his error, placed the table top in a new location, where it immediately fell to the ground. Once we all had settled in, speeches were made to congratulate Maria, she said a prayer, and the food was served. Having already eaten dinner, I was not at all hungry, but, not wanting to refuse, I slowly shoveled what I could into my mouth for the next half hour. Eventually, a young woman named Rita removed my plate. Noticing that I had succeeded in eating most of the food, she asked, "You didn't give your food to someone else, did you?"

After eating, Maria received some gifts, and then the dancing began. At the risk of making a generalization, Ugandans can dance. Even the little children have rhythm. My own ability is far inferior, and I avoid dancing at all costs. But, after remaining stoically seated for a few minutes, my neighbors prevailed upon me, and I rose to join in. I do not claim to have impressed anyone that night, but I will admit that dancing in the moonlight with these friends and neighbors was fun. Being invited to take part in this celebration is something I will always remember.

After leaving the guest house and walking the short distance to my front door, I took a few moments to reflect on the experience. What I found most striking was the sense of accomplishment that had permeated the group. It was not only felt by Maria, but by her friends and family as well, as if it were a team effort. And truly, I'm sure it was. It seemed obvious to me that Maria had been accompanied by a loving family, a loyal group of friends, and supportive teachers on her road to graduation.

During those nights spent in my old bedroom, I found myself recalling Maria and her family. I found myself thinking of Prossy's children, Suzan's children, and Max's children – all at very different stages of their lives, but all having loving and supportive networks propelling them forward. I have that, too, and I can't begin to imagine how my life would have been different without it. It took so many people to help me through the relatively minor trials of my own life. But some people don't have these things. Some people don't have a warm and welcoming home that is always open. Some people don't find themselves within a surrounding atmosphere of hope and love. Those nights spent in my old bedroom, I sometimes found myself thinking of them, wondering what, if anything, I could do, and asking of the darkness, "How many people sleep tonight with only you surrounding them?"

Silent Lullabies

A homecoming fraught with frigid bones
And frozen tears not falling,
The crackle, beneath my feet, of stones
I've known since timid crawling,
Leads me to the welcome door
Containing love assuring.

Inside I recall the sounds of days
Now faded, faintly ringing,
As crackling stove, with warming blaze,
Allays the cold air's stinging;
Sweet remembered chords we strum
That thaw my fingers' numbing.

But as I extinguish bedroom's light,
All wrapped in peace resounding,
Consider the ones, this chilling night,
Who feel no love surrounding.
Sing them silent lullabies
Of warmth and hope abounding,
For no one at home truly lies,
Till all can hear them sounding.

During those six wintry weeks, my days were spent relaxing and, often, becoming reacquainted with my cello and piano. True, I could have been working on my thesis, but I knew I would have time for that once I returned to Florida in January. And so, many of my days were filled with music. Some days were less successful than others, as my hands and fingertips, so long away from these instruments, slowly remembered the correct movements and regained their stamina. But most of the time, I realized how much I had missed it while in Uganda, and I recalled why I so love the opportunity to make music. I rediscovered that feeling – the feeling of sound growing in the air around me and blossoming in my heart, expanding to connect us with our surroundings, as it reveals the depths of truth that are there but are too profound for words. For me, it can be a transcendent experience.

I didn't really forget about the beauty and value of music in Uganda. Rather, I think I simply missed the full experience of its creation and development. But at the same time, occasional reminders restored and rejuvenated my passion and wonder for it. An experience from my first few months in the country comes to mind, when I was in training and living with the Katambas, my host family in Wakiso.

Over the weeks I spent with them, I had begun to form a small bond with Hosea, the youngest child in the house. Many evenings, tentatively at first but more confidently with time, he would walk into my room while I was reading or reviewing the day's Luganda lessons. We would pick up one of the picture books I had brought with me (and which I would eventually give to him when my time with this family was complete). We would open it on my bed, he would point to the objects that populated the pages, and I would say their names in English. Then, we would switch roles. Often, his mom or one of his sisters would have to drag him away when it was time for all of us to go to sleep.

One evening, while I was sitting at the dinner table, Robin, my host mother, was playing with Hosea nearby. She then noticed someone outside in the front yard and went out to talk. Hosea remained inside and seemed to become very worried about her, perhaps wondering whether or not she would come back. Of course, she was just outside, and we could hear her talking. Even so, he began to bawl – quite loudly. I started to talk to him, trying to use English and my limited Luganda to reassure him. These efforts were unsuccessful, so I walked over to where he was standing, picked him up, brought him back to the table, and sat down with him in my lap. I continued talking to him, attempting to use my most calming, soothing voice, as he continued to cry without a shred of calm.

Eventually, I changed tactics. As I held him in my lap, I started to sway gently back and forth, and I began humming a lullaby. Almost immediately, Hosea was silent. The tears ceased, and he simply listened. Repeating the lullaby, he stayed calm for several minutes, as Robin finished her conversation and returned to the house. When she entered, I let Hosea down, and he ran to her, while I thoughtfully finished supper.

Music has a universal quality to it. It's difficult to explain and sometimes difficult to see, especially when one begins to consider the drastically different characteristics of the music that emanates from various cultures. And yet, that quality is there, going deeper into ourselves while at the same time expanding beyond boundaries and borders. A beautiful melody – or my rough, attempted rendition of one – seems to touch us somewhere beyond the cultural differences we might see on the outside. We can all appreciate, enjoy, and love the wonderful music existing in the sound waves that traverse the air around us.

Think about how sound is created. In a very literal sense, it connects those creating it with those listening to it. Whether in a concert hall or in a small dining room, the sound waves radiating from the musicians stretch out to reach the listeners, touching both groups and allowing them all to share in the experience, each in his or her own way.

Before living in Uganda, I loved music, but saw it as an exquisite luxury, as something unlikely to contribute to the practical lives of those in difficult situations. I see it differently today. Now, I wonder if, perhaps, music can help us all to find the common humanity within every person, to bring us together as we realize that we are not so different after all. As I sat at that dinner table, struggling to understand a culture which, at the time, seemed so foreign to me, I was able to connect, at least for a few minutes, with a little boy from that culture, simply by singing a calm and peaceful tune. It seemed to transcend any cultural boundaries that might have been at work. It bound us together and stilled our souls.

As distinct individuals, we each find our deepest selves and our most fundamental connections in some unique combination of things – in music, in poetry, in art, in service, or through still other avenues. These things that are less concrete and less tangible are no less important. They help us to discover the truth and the splendor that are sometimes so difficult to see in this hurried, uncertain, and flawed world. They ignite in us a sense of wonder and a deep awareness of the beauty that lies within ourselves, within others, and within the world around us. Without that wonder, we are simply speeding down a highway, oblivious to the stirrings of the soul as it searches for meaning. Without the beauty of life, we lock our hearts in an empty box, devoid of the connections that make life worth living.

It's something different for everyone, but, for me, music unchains my soul and draws me closer to that beauty, to God, and to the essence of existence. I touch the keys of the piano and see a gray world turn to color. I lift the cello from its case, draw the bow across the strings, and feel the pull of something originating far beyond my sight.

Moments of Music

Years away,
Spent in another place,
Fade into your sound upon this day,
When opened is your case.
Notes array,
Summer wind, autumn leaves,
Winter's freeze, and flower blooms of May,
Caressed, my ear receives
What you say.
I listen as you grow,
Bold crescendo, rising, golden ray,
I feel you grip the bow.
Silence lay
After the last note rang,
Fingers touching chords that fade away,
And then my spirit sang,
Rose to pray,
For moments when I feel
Drawn to all existence to display
Your melodies that heal,
When I play.

As the new year began, I left my parent's house in Pennsylvania and moved to Florida, where I would spend the next few months finishing my thesis. The days and weeks passed quickly, and, although my mind was constantly thinking about my work in Uganda, the immediacy of my feelings about the experience began to fade. The fog of elapsing time slowly grew, as my thoughts focused on the analysis of my results, the intricacies of technical writing, and the possibilities for my future. Was I starting to lose the lessons, the truths, and the perspectives I had been shown, as I returned to my own path of academic focus? Was my own perspective becoming clouded, as those lessons slipped away?

Occasionally, my memory would be refreshed by a message from one of my former coworkers or by the photographs I was sifting through as I worked on my final presentation. As more time passed, these images became a way for me to refill my soul, riding waves of nostalgia back to the memories of my time in Uganda. But, at the same time, these memories felt incomplete and simplified. I sometimes felt as if I were only remembering certain aspects of the experience, splitting and delineating events into easy categories – good or bad, simple or hard, smooth or rough, peaceful or turbulent.

I began to wonder about my own filters through which I see, consider, and remember the world. Do they oversimplify events and experiences, sorting and reforming them into discrete categories and monothematic impressions? Admittedly, part of me went to Uganda searching for and expecting simplicity – problems to solve, people to help, my own life to streamline. In truth, what I found tended more toward complexity, toward a layered existence full of hidden connections. Almost everything I've experienced, whether in Uganda or somewhere else, has been a mixture of different parts, rarely classifiable as wholly good or bad. Were my memories causing me to revert back to my previous conceptions? Could I maintain that sense of intricacy, of interdependence, of ambiguity, which had shown itself so clearly in Uganda?

Filtered Memories

My life, a vein of hot and cold,
Of light and dark, of new and old,
Through which the mixtures run.
But glancing back, appearing pure,
The mingled natures scarce endure,
Complexities undone.
Could depth be lost, when, like a sieve,
I keep just part of what I live:
This action bad, that other, good,
Am I not seeing what I should?
Or is it like the sun?
Would I go blind beneath the load?
In paradox, could mind explode?

To gaze sustained upon the truth,
For this I've yearned since former youth.
And yet a merely fleeting glance
Could scorch my soul and stay my chance
To take my filtered memories,
Restore their subtle harmonies,
And see the web full-spun.
Perhaps it's more than I can know,
This working of the greater flow,
Of which I am but one small drop
Whose borders, yet, seem not to stop:
Infinity in one.

As I look back on my time in Florida, I realize now that I felt somewhat transient while there, both in the year before I left for Uganda and in the months after I returned. As with other places in my life up to this point, Florida was a location where I spent a passing span of time, waiting for the next phase, the next stopping point on my journey. This is not to say that I didn't meet wonderful people there. I did, but, perhaps due to this temporary feeling, I never felt a true connection to the place.

On top of that, my Peace Corps service seemed to function as a dividing line in my life, with my experiences before it feeling different from those after it. Three years in Uganda changed many things about the way I see the world, and, especially given the limited connection I had felt during my previous year in Florida, returning there this past year felt less like a homecoming and more like something unfamiliar. In stark contrast to the rootedness – the sense of home – I had felt in Uganda and at my parents' house, some part of me experienced Florida as if I were floating through it, slightly apart, knowing that I would leave again soon.

But there was still more to it than that. In my nearly singular focus on the analysis and presentation of my research, I was not allowing myself to reach out to the world at hand, and to touch it as it touched me. Uganda brought the challenges and difficulties of life, the sometimes strained, always imperfect connections with one another and with our environment, into immediate focus. While there, I could ignore them for brief periods. If I wanted to, I could shut myself in my house and be alone with my thoughts, but this situation could not persist for long. Life would come knocking at my door. It would force me to walk the streets and interact with the life outside of my own. It was full of complexity, a varied tapestry of joyful mountaintops interwoven with valleys of doubt, uncertainty, and struggle. But it was also full of truth.

I see now that, in some ways, my time in Florida may have been an extended valley – not so much a deep chasm, but more of a gently sloping dip in my life's landscape. It had nothing to do with the people there or with the place itself. It was completely due to my own mindset, my own gradual realization that, after leaving Uganda, I had left a place and a group of people that I had come to love. That love was not a trivial emotion that comes from only remembering an experience's pleasant qualities, but a deeper appreciation that has come through its difficulties and knows that the fullness of the experience would be less without those struggles.

And so, in Florida, I allowed my focus to become so narrow, so rarefied, that I could push everything else out. I forgot some of the wonder, some of the reverence for the world outside of me, as I sat in front of the computer, disconnected from my surroundings. It was nearly impossible to fall into that trap in Uganda, but it was all too easy after returning. Occasionally, I would take a break, losing myself in the nostalgia of photographs and the love of a life that had gone from me.

Memories' Replies

From where, beneath the sky's gray, shrouded guise,
From where do these bright memories arise?
In fuzzy sight, they brush across my eyes,
As 'cross my skin run wind's slight, toneless sighs.
Upon the ground, the sounds of rain surprise,
Restore my dreams to streams that wander nigh,
But one small thought still lingers, underlies,
And wonders if your heart hears and replies.

One evening, as I looked up from the computer and walked to the window, I started to understand. As I listened to the natural sounds that had been too long forgotten, my soul began to reawaken. My memories were not simply pulling me back toward something in the past. They were pushing me forward, inviting me to consider what I had learned and to use it in my next steps. My time in Uganda was a turning point in my life, not a stopping point. There is always more to discover. There is always further to go.

That experience, which I had been so fortunate to have, taught me so much about life, and I now have a responsibility to use that knowledge, wherever I happen to be. It's not simply an obligation – the more I think about it, the more I realize that it's a desire, even a need. I find myself feeling drawn, inexorably, to the life outside of my window, to the environment that sustains me, to the other souls I find near me. I am pushed, and, somewhere deep in my soul, I yearn, to step out into their midst. What will I find?

Remember to Look Out the Window

I seldom walk in silence with the stars,
Shutting out the night with lamps a-glowing.
I find myself inside a box too narrow,
Cutting off the call to mystic knowing.
But once I walked, and felt the healing scars,
Seeing not from where the balm was flowing.
It drew me deep, though now I wander shallow,
Inner seedlings stunted in their growing.

Remember to look out the window.
Remember to walk in the dark.
There is wisdom there, in the shadow,
And wonder enlivens her spark.
Escape from the insular life
Of ceilings and light bulbs and doors,
To return to steps under starlight,
Where essence expands and restores.

In the looking, in the searching, in the rekindled awareness of my surroundings, a sense of complexity began to reemerge. As I finished my work in Florida and returned that summer to my family in Pennsylvania, my thoughts began to turn toward issues larger and, perhaps, more meaningful than the ultra-focused pinpricks of knowledge my research had explored. Climate change, environmental degradation, national and global political conflict, refugee crises, food security, water scarcity, health, local and global poverty – these are just some of the broad, interconnected, multifaceted concerns that we face as the world rushes onward. These are matters that require people from diverse backgrounds and perspectives to come together, to cross borders and boundaries, and to build solutions out of the relationships that are created.

And yet, we still sometimes focus on what divides us, rather than what unites us. We still sometimes dismiss the perspectives of others, if their experiences and ideas do not coincide with our own. I've returned to the United States at a time of much anger, and some of that anger involves issues of race.

I grew up not thinking a great deal about race. The local area was certainly not completely devoid of members of minority groups, but it was a predominantly white area, and I attended schools with predominantly white student populations. In 2008, during my second year of college, I watched President Obama's inauguration, perhaps seeing it as a proof that the country had progressed beyond the sins of slavery and segregation, that the voices of those who were previously oppressed and marginalized were now being fully heard. As revealed by the voices that have recently swept through many parts of the United States, the true story is not so complete, not so neatly concluded.

I can never fully comprehend, on a visceral and emotional level, the life experiences of minorities in the United States. But perhaps, as a result of my own experiences and interactions in Uganda, I have been given a window through which I can more clearly see small pieces of those experiences. There, I found myself firmly in the minority. Because of the color of my skin and the place of my birth, certain assumptions were made about me, and these could lead to misunderstandings and uncomfortable situations. It's important to note that, in my case, the assumptions were generally quite different from those that might be attached to minorities in the United States, and, as a last resort if things became too difficult, the option for me to leave was always open. For some volunteers, whose negative experiences were more acute than mine, leaving became a viable possibility. For me, fortunately, it never needed to be seriously considered, but I still felt the sting of slanted and distorted assumptions.

Due to parts of myself that I considered to be superficial, I was often perceived as having large amounts of wealth, influence, and power. This was not the case, but, at least during initial meetings, others saw me in this way. Although it was rarely stated explicitly, I also occasionally found myself being seen as an outsider, as one who did not quite belong. To walk down the street and to feel the eyes tracking, watching and evaluating my every move, to be seen as a representative of an entire race or of the entire population of a country, was overwhelming and exhausting. It was heavy. It's not a burden I wanted.

There are those in the United States who have grown up with these feelings, who have felt that weight for their entire lives, who know, so much better than I do, what it means to be seen as "The Other". These people do not have the option, as I did, to fly away or to console themselves with the knowledge that, soon, they will be returning to a place of safety, security, and comfort. And there is so much more to their experience that I have not known. I cannot begin to pretend that my own dealings have shown me the full extent of the struggle imposed on those who have been marginalized and oppressed by personal, everyday actions of physical and mental violence and by the expansive structures of accumulated power. But perhaps I have, in an extremely limited way, come to better understand pieces of that struggle and of the people who find themselves in the midst of it. Theirs are the voices we must hear. We must respect and honor their stories. They have lived those stories, and it is too often too easy for those of us who have not inhabited those lives to brush them aside.

Over the past few years, I have been learning about and extolling the virtues of diversity. I have focused less on the potential difficulties in getting to a point where diversity is an accepted and desired part of our lives, although I have seen and felt the seeds of those difficulties in my experiences across two continents. I cannot claim to have a solution to the manifold boundaries and injustices that continue to plague society, to the historical persistence of prejudices and the oppressive structures they produce and embolden. But it must begin in listening to one another with love and empathy, and especially in hearing those whose voices have not always been heard. In them lies truth that can adjust or augment our own views of the world, and in the conversation lies hope.

Disarming Love

Rage,
Uncaged and running red with fury
Past the bodies yet to bury,
Gunshots ringing through the alley,
Mothers, choking, crushed by worry,
Pray the drums won't raise the tally:
"Stop! Be still, don't turn the page…"

One million tiny candles brightly
Burning in the night,
And though the anger grips them tightly,
No, they will not turn to fight.
The pain of years on each clenched fist is etched,
A violent, rugged glove,
Advancing, now, with open hands outstretched
In strong, disarming love.

MOVEMENT 11 | LOVING

Grounded Constellations

High in the sky, the light crystals fly,
Pulsing with bright luminations.
Through night's veil they slide, ignited inside,
By atoms' infused combinations.
Though light-years divide, our eyes have applied
Relations and representations.
Alignment invites a sighting of sprites,
Heroes, and mythic creations.

Down on the ground, the towering sound
Of never-fulfilled expectations,
Surrounding us now, the powerful growl
Impels us with no explanations.
With no space to slow the flow of the show,
To celebrate life's fascinations,
No rest to reflect, no chance to connect,
Has awe joined forgotten sensations?

Is wonder now dead for stars overhead,
When glancing from our grounded stations?
If we could but see, they mirror the key
To charting our souls' explorations.
A light we each hide, invisibly tied

To others and new revelations.
So why don't we fly, and rise with a sigh
To calmer, deep-breathed elevations?

A relentless barrage of sound and stimuli overwhelms our senses. At least, that is how I feel sometimes, with an array of electronic windows open and actively vying for my attention, as real windows, away from computer screens, are so easily neglected. We expound upon our thoughts, speaking in a virtual environment, in an insulated, narrow box, perhaps forgetting that life is to be lived out there, rather than portrayed in here. Reality and truth are to be found in the spontaneous symphony of the natural world, in the profound stillness of the composed mind, and in the presence of souls in relationship with one another. It is in these places that we might find a love that could change the world.

I am as guilty as anyone else, and perhaps more so. I have had opportunities to see this world and the people in it from a different angle. Yet, I continue to find myself falling back, regressing into the familiarity of a life lived without that alternative perspective, of an unmindful existence chronically distracted by the moment's minutiae at the expense of deeper reflection. In this frenzied environment, it can become easy to dismiss the humanity of others – to forget that the experiences of others have as much value as my own.

How do we return? How might we find our way back to an ever-present mindset that simultaneously acknowledges differences and commonalities, that truly loves and sees the beauty in this world, in others, and in ourselves?

For me, music remains one way to catch glimpses of this state of mind, as does being present in the natural world. My few years in Uganda highlighted the value of experiencing nature. I was occasionally forced to look around and take it all in. It would be incorrect to call Uganda an idyllic, pristine environment that allows for constant meditation. But, through some combination of nature, people, and the whispers of my own mind, that place did reveal to me the value of solitude with one's own thoughts, the value of communion with nature, and the value of an undistracted openness that enables pure focus on the person standing in front of me. Sometimes, the realizations were aided by what seemed at the time to be inconveniences – a lack of electricity, internet access, phone service, or other things some of us take for granted. At other times, they were helped along by the people and places I encountered.

It is this type of experience that can remind us of the wonder of this life, and of an appropriate sense of awe. This past summer, after leaving Florida, I spent some more time with my family in Pennsylvania. At one point, my mother and I took a trip to the northern part of the state, filled with meandering streams, well-worn forests, and rolling mountains shaped by ancient time. In one of the state parks where we stopped, we walked along a high trail overlooking a deep gorge. We came to a point where a clearing in the trees allowed a breathtaking view of the slopes and the river below. As I stood there, with my hands resting on a wooden railing, an orange and black butterfly began to flutter close to my right shoe. It landed there and remained for a few minutes before gently returning to the air.

Later, on a different trail in the same area, a butterfly with a very similar appearance once again came close to me, this time resting on the back of my bare hand. I doubt that it was the same butterfly, but the resemblance, to my untrained eyes, was striking. As its wings slowly opened and closed, I found myself considering the connections that can cross even differences between species, as one life reaches out to another life and draws it closer. I know it is somewhat irrational to find universal lessons in the simple actions of one or two butterflies. But, these ideas have also blossomed out of a long process that began with some of the initial questions of my life: What can I do to improve the world? How can I make an impact? As the butterfly quietly took its leave, the various lessons of my past began to coalesce.

Nature forgives. Our actions, on a local scale as well as on a global scale, have harmed the environment in which we live. How many butterflies have we injured? How many trees have we felled? How many animals have learned to avoid us if at all possible? How many species have we lost because of our recklessness, or at least our lack of awareness? Nature has absorbed it all and continues to reach out to us, calling us back toward a positive relationship. The butterflies return to our hands. Nature forgives.

We could all use a little more forgiveness. We could all use a little more awareness of the connections with our world and with one another. We could all use a little more openness to take part in a conversation characterized by understanding and love.

But let's be clear about what true forgiveness is. It's not simply one party apologizing while the other party responds, "It is forgiven." The peace and reconciliation that can come from true forgiveness require a change in the attitudes on both sides, a movement away from confrontation and toward cooperation. This process does not necessarily eliminate the possibility of consequences or penalties for wrongdoing, but the end goal is not retribution for crimes committed or payment of a debt owed. The goal is a changed connection, a turning of negative attitudes into positive ones – into a restored relationship. It is not easy, but true forgiveness is a core aspect of love that could change the world.

We could all use a little more forgiveness and a little more understanding of "The Other". It has become too easy for us to walk down the road and to render invisible those we do not wish to see. Again, I am guilty of this offense. In Uganda, I would often walk past people begging on the street. It was more common in Kampala, but it also happened in Kalisizo. Many of these people were obviously stricken with physical disabilities or with mental illness. While it was frequently stressed that we as Peace Corps Volunteers should not hand out money to these people, I did at least try to make a point of looking these people in the eye and smiling, if for no other reason than to show them, and perhaps to prove to myself, that I saw them as valuable human beings. But, there were still times when I cowardly looked the other way, pretending not to notice the person sitting on the sidewalk – pretending that the person was not there, that the person did not exist. At these times, I contributed to the dehumanization of that person.

I think the important thing for us to remember, whether in Uganda, the United States, or somewhere else, is that we don't know the circumstances that brought that person to this point. We don't know if he or she was simply unlucky, if a personal loss created a devastating change in his or her life, or if some other factor was at work. I truly believe that we are more alike than we often perceive. Given different circumstances, each of us might find ourselves in a similar situation. Even if those in desperate circumstances did make significant mistakes, is it not possible to also see ourselves making similar errors, under certain conditions? It is a fine line we walk, and I know that I, at least, can easily wander off course. The moral quality of each of our souls is neither wholly good nor utterly evil. We are all painted a shade of gray, existing somewhere between a perfect heaven and a depraved hell. Our own ambiguity could help us to better understand those we may wish to keep out of sight, to forgive them for any wrongs they may have committed, to realize that being in a desperate situation does not automatically prove that any mistakes were actually made, and to restore their relationships with the community.

And yet, in reality, we often continue to push these people away. What will it take for us to see these "Others" as human beings like ourselves, all of us flawed yet precious, all in need of compassion and love, not judgment or indifference? Could we, today, take measures to reach out to these people on the margins, and to invite them back into restored connections? Or, like the grain of wheat in the parable, will they remain cut off, disconnected until death, only then showing us what we have missed, showing us how our actions have not lived up to the words we have spoken about love and forgiveness?

A Grain of Wheat

They found me in the street when sunrise broke,
Lying there alone, beneath a shredded, sweaty cloak.
They said it was a stroke that had struck the night before,
But I wonder, could it be something more?

My dad, he owned a store in our hometown.
Funds were often short, I wished for more than father's crown,
But mother stopped each frown that had crept across my face,
As she whispered, "Work hard, you'll find your place."

And so I ran the race we're told to run:
Went away to school, another wide-eyed, eager son,
Then wished it to be done and to rest my furrowed brow,
While I pondered, "I hope I'll make it now."

I'd heard some tales of how to start careers:
Find a first-rung job and climb the ladder up the years.
To outperform one's peers, one must give one's life to work,
So I promised, "My duties I'll not shirk."

How close disasters lurk when all seems fine.
Just a breath away, and then the stars fall out of line.
This path so surely mine had been taken, reassigned.
Costs were rising, so I was left behind.

This crushing state of mind I tried to hide,
Oh, but fate denied, for that same week my mother died.
I felt so cold inside, while my father cried with grief,
Always soothing, her words now no relief.

My heart a shriveled leaf, remaining money spent,
All to care for Dad, whose mind was now forever bent.
I could not pay the rent, I was thrown out on the street.
Broken, lonely, I begged for scraps to eat.

Perhaps you know the rest, for though the years crawled by,
I never left the weight that pressed upon my weary eye.
There's nothing more to say; one night in pain I fell,
Though every day I'd heard you pray and speak of love so well.

But where were you when profits trumped my life?
And where were you when Mother felt death's knife?
This tale is not your fault, nor is it mine.
You cannot straighten every crooked line.
But this love of which you speak might have eased fate's icy shriek,
As it pierced my deepest shell and filled me with a bleak, cold hell.

Or, if that love were shared still more,
Would sweeping changes be in store?
Would truth be spoken?
Would chains be broken
That keep us all, in some way, poor?

How much could love achieve if it were shared still more? What physical and spiritual deficits could it heal? These questions relate to an internal debate that often surfaced while in Uganda: Is it more important to help people meet their physical needs or to satisfy their spiritual needs – the need to belong, to feel loved and accepted, to see the beauty present in the world, in others, and in ourselves?

I went to Uganda thinking that the sphere of development work was mostly focused on building things. While I certainly acknowledged the importance of working together with local partners and communities, I was mostly concerned with meeting physical needs, so that those people could lead lives that were healthier and more economically secure. I suppose my argument was that people cannot truly be free to live fulfilling and fruitful lives if the basic necessities are unavailable, and that it can be very difficult, if not impossible, to escape conditions of severe poverty if at least a few of these essentials are not in place – things like access to clean water supplies, safe sanitation facilities, and decent classrooms where children can learn.

I still believe this line of reasoning contains truth, but I also know now that there is more to the story. Over the past few years, I've come to better understand that the needs and health of the soul are at least as important as material needs, and that the soul has a profound impact on the overall wellbeing of the self and others. People who appear to have little in the way of material wealth may have abundant stores of moral virtue and radiant, inspirational energy. In many ways, they may be far more "developed" than I am. We all have something to teach one another.

When I left Uganda, I had come to believe that sincere and effective development work is more about building relationships, rather than things. It's about strengthening the connections that help us to learn about – and to learn from – one another. Material wellbeing remains vitally important, but the wellbeing of the soul is primary.

To be clear, when referring to spiritual wellbeing, I have in mind this life's immediate reality, a reality in which souls could find a sense of deep belonging and discover the beauty contained within ourselves and the world around us. It's not simply a superficial attempt to make us all a bit nicer and happier. It could have significant implications that transcend the limited physical reach of our outstretched arms. Here and now, at this present moment, the material and the spiritual intersect within each of us, and the enigmatic energy of the soul can profoundly impact our everyday lives.

Out of these interactions between souls, relationships can form that lead naturally toward a shared desire to improve the physical wellbeing of those whose basic needs are not being met. When approached from this direction, when ideas for development can grow organically out of these meaningful personal connections, I think the work we do together is likely to be more contextually appropriate, more readily accepted by the local community, and more useful for everyone involved. It is built on a greater foundation of mutual trust and respect. It is based on the idea that, while physical essentials are important for a person's wellbeing, life is more than material security and comfort. Through a combined respect for the material and the spiritual, with the connections of our souls forming the underlying foundation, progress that is true, lasting, and holistic might be achieved.

Soul Shakers

Earth shakers, ground breakers, brick bakers, bridge makers,
I once had thought that I was one of these,
To build, to bring to those in need
The physical necessities.

Somewhere between those thoughts and now,
Viewpoints that had seemed so clean
Adjusted, turned to plough
Other tracks, somehow:
A deeper scene,
Heart and brow,
Restless now,
Someday will be serene.

Tangible needs are vital still:
Water, shelter from the heat and chill,
And food enough for all to have their fill.
Lack thereof, a symptom of a greater ill,
Of shrunken spirits left upon the windowsill,
Dormant from disuse of love, a long-neglected quill.

Soul shakers, risk takers, heart quakers, mind wakers,
I feel my spirit drawn to inner tone,
Awakening love's voices from the silence.
Will you help me find my own?

This focus on the inner life of the soul requires, or is at least aided by, an important, yet often fleeting ability – the ability to be fully present in the current moment. Especially in the context of the hurried, multifaceted environments where we often find ourselves, effort is needed to focus attention solely on the present conversation, the present line of contemplation, or whatever concern presents itself before us. It's so easy for the mind to wander, for thoughts to turn away from the immediate needs of the moment. And yet, I see this ability as another crucial component of a love that could change the world.

It is relatively simple to discuss the qualities of love within the safety and comfort of words, abstract concepts, and hypotheticals. The true measure of love can be seen in the reaction to the present reality, in its active manifestation when faced with an immediate concern. In the moment, my theories become like empty shells if my actions do not live up to my ideals – if my response to a person standing before me in need of love is not all that it should be. Only in action can the true nature of love be realized, and only through the impulse of an unexpected encounter can we truly see the content of our hearts. In these moments, the person takes precedence over any other consideration. The relationship must be primary, with love transcending doctrine, opinion, ritual, and the laws that we construct for ourselves and try to follow. Only by being wholly present in the moment can the relationship be fully realized.

During many moments in my life, and especially in Uganda, I have found my own loving responses to be lacking. Despite the consideration I have given to the concept of love, my active expression of it has often been far from perfect. Fortunately for me, the lives of others have demonstrated a thoughtful and selfless love that has helped me to learn. Their lives have shown me how this selfless love nourishes others as well as the self, strengthening the relationships between people and the bonds that link us to the outside world.

I met a man in Uganda named Eric, a retired priest living in Rukungiri, a town in the southwestern part of the country. He now spends his days promoting environmentally sound sanitation and hygiene in his community. In the middle of my service, I spent a few days in his community, working with him and two other Peace Corps Volunteers to conduct a survey among users of Eco-San systems, which are much more common and familiar in Rukungiri than they are in Kalisizo. We ended up writing a paper about it, which we submitted to an international conference on water, sanitation, and hygiene. As a result, Eric had the opportunity to travel to Kenya, where he presented the work.

Eric truly practices what he preaches. At his home just outside of town, Eco-San systems are installed, and he uses the products in his garden. One night, I ate dinner at his house, a dinner filled with vegetables from that garden, and it was some of the best food I ate during my three years in Uganda. Although, physically, I spent less than a week with him, Eric has become one of my favorite people from my time in Uganda. His sense of humor is wonderful, and his dedication to environmental stewardship and community well-being is inspiring. He undoubtedly has something of value to say. His voice is important in this world.

As with so many times in my life, I was not always completely present during these events. It is often the case that the mind feels as if it wants to go in several different directions, recalling the past, planning for the future, and thinking of people and things who are somewhere else. I probably did not fully appreciate Eric's presence when I was with him, and it would have been all too easy for our connection to end when I left Rukungiri. Fortunately, however, due in large part to Eric's efforts, we have stayed in contact over the months since I left, and I'm glad that the relationship has continued. In this regard, I have to appreciate the vast reach of the internet across so much of the world, helping to prevent the fading of these types of relationships, although they remain dependent on the initiative of each person.

As it turned out, while I was in Florida, we worked together to write another paper. And again, Eric was able to travel to an international conference, this time in London, to give a presentation about these topics for which he has so much passion. He recently sent me an email telling me about the time he and his wife were able to spend there, and about the conference itself, where I am sure he gave an incredible presentation.

I know it's such a small thing, to work on these papers with Eric. He has usually supplied most of the basic content, while I have simply helped to organize it, to put it into a broader context, and to tell the story. I have enjoyed these collaborations very much, but I'd like to think that there is a bit more to it than that. I'd like to think that, in some small way, I am beginning to put what I have learned into practice, to work toward amplifying the voice of another and enabling its message and its heart to reach a broader audience. Many people could benefit from what Eric has to say. What more could we do to highlight the voices and perspectives of Eric and of others who have so much to offer the world?

As our own inner voices struggle to penetrate an endless flood of incessant noise, I wonder if the support and consideration of others' voices are things we tend to overlook. And yet, they are crucial. In the presence of another soul, being lovingly present means listening to the other's voice. It means focusing intently on the words, on the perspectives, on the life of this unique individual. Similarly, being able to truly forgive another is helped by this same openness. Being able to see a person's flawed humanity, and to connect it with one's own, is helped by this willingness to hear the other's story firsthand without judgment. We are not here to judge one another. We are here to tend the tree of love.

As we amplify the voices of others from diverse backgrounds, as we open our own minds to those voices and allow them to work in us, as our love for others grows through our heightened understanding and awareness of the souls standing before us, perhaps we will find the fruit of that tree to be a peace greater than any we have ever known – a peace, running through ourselves and the world around us, that surpasses our understanding.

The Fruit of the Tree of Love

One, all alone, as silent as stone,
Sends out a call to the essence of all:
"Where might we find a peace that will shine
Through our souls for all time?"

The silence deepens, night falls outside,
Patiently waiting, but still no answer nigh.
Silently, faithfully,
In the solitude, sitting subdued,
With the stars above, she starts thinking of
How the fruit of a faithful prayer is love.

Rising up from the ground,
Seeing life all around,
As she runs to the love she has found.

Touching a part of eternity's heart
Within a love that is lit from above,
Where might it lead after planting the seed?
What will come of the tree?

Roots of connection spread love through the earth,
Leaves of compassion sing forth our human worth,
Branches strong, reaching long
Into distant lands, she understands:
Let our hatred cease, let our fears release,
For the fruit of the tree of love is peace.

Yes, within these beloved hearts is peace.

The potential for this peace exists within us and within our relationships. Yet, it continues to remain elusive. All this talk of connection suggests a fundamental, philosophical question, one that may contribute to the gulf between our current reality and our ideals. Are we discrete, individual units within this vast system of space and time, or are we connected elements within a greater whole? Do we each strike out along a unique course, or do we find ourselves sharing the road with others?

It's almost certainly some amalgamation of the two. Along the continuum between these two extremes, we each likely have our own idea of our true position. We each have our own thoughts on whether, in general, we are characterized more by individuality or collectivity, whether the lives we lead are more akin to unique paths or shared courses. There is a tension between these two poles – a tension that seems to be an important piece of at least some of the enduring disagreements with which we perpetually struggle.

Each side of the coin has value and a ring of truth. The distinctive perspective and creative force within each soul allow that individual to bring something different – something wholly new – to any moment, to any point in space and time. Then again, those perspectives are partially dependent upon our relationships with one another, and, all across the canvas of creation, the tightly-woven brushstrokes of interdependency are evident. Our true state within this universe is some ambiguous mixture of these two concepts, while at the same time being so much more than the sum of two competing philosophical theories.

I don't claim to know exactly where we fall within this uncertain framework. Even if, somehow, I did know, I couldn't then claim to immediately understand how that knowledge should be applied in every specific situation. But, even so, based on what our experiences have taught us – based on the wisdom handed down through the people of our past, the trees of the forest, the depths of the sea, and the whispers of our hearts – perhaps we can still say something of value regarding this topic.

Maybe the question is not meant to be reduced down to one choice or another, to one point that defines the nature of life and the level of connection between us all. Perhaps the question's complexity is what gives it power, a power that could push us all to do better, to think harder, and to love more. In many ways, our lives are shaped by our uncertainty of who and what we are, and that uncertainty can propel us forward on our quest to improve ourselves, our world, and our understanding. In the end, the lives of meaning we strive for – lives filled with love, learning, and beauty – need both extremes. They need to be capable of emphasizing the worth of the individual standing right in front of us, as well as the value of the broad community that binds us all together.

A love that could change the world always treats the life of an individual who is immediately before us as the most important in the universe. It is totally present, it is always supporting and listening intently, and it is ever-ready to forgive or to ask for forgiveness with a humble heart. Only in this love is the true value of the individual fully realized. At the same time, only in this love are the strongest connections within the community built and reinforced.

At this time when it is so easy to talk past one another, when we find it so difficult to believe others to be completely genuine, when we read about, hear about, and see too many examples of people whose actions do not match their words, perhaps this active yet gentle love is one truly effective way to shed light on a different path. Although, often, I did not notice the specific moment when it happened, I now see, looking back, how the love of others found its way inside of me and started to change my own heart. This is what true love can do. It gets inside of you, it works its way into the soil of your soul, and there it begins to sprout and grow. This is love's power – give it, and create more.

It is not an empty gesture. It does not stop at clichéd words and simple platitudes. It is a daring commitment, one that I am continually trying to make, always imperfectly. It is a love that fills in the cracks, that resides in the margins, that encompasses all who have been forgotten or left aside, that reminds everyone it encounters of the beauty within his or her own soul. It embraces and lives out the idea that we all deserve love, from the least to the greatest, from the poor to the rich, from the sick to the healthy – people of all stripes, all colors, all races, all religions. We are each inherently valuable.

And yet, in a universe of stars and planets and galaxies beyond the reach of our dreams, we are small. Still, embedded in a vast community filled with relationships, in our smallness lies potential greatness. The love that looks beyond one's self plants its seeds in the hearts of all it touches, and it begins to spread. It grows slowly, for love is a longer road. It takes time to form relationships. It takes time to engender trust and illuminate the truths within our souls. But as it grows, new voices take up its call. Connections solidify, drawing us closer to one another and to the foundation, the source of life and love at the heart of everything. As if we are remembering something from a time before our rational understanding took shape, we begin to realize that our lives become fuller when more voices – those of the silenced, the distressed, the different – are added to the chorus. Our broken and bent relationships begin to heal.

Only love can create this wholesale change of heart. Only changed hearts can lead to true peace – a peace not built on law, force, or compulsion, but on kindness, thoughtfulness, and love. It is an ideal, a community that may seem unattainable and is placed farther out of reach with every act of hate, violence, or indifference. We cannot help but humbly acknowledge our smallness in the face of such towering odds. But there is greatness in our smallness, for love is an infinite quantity. One individual with a true heart, acting out of love, can pour out that love onto others, filling the souls of everyone involved. Each of us is like a shard of a mirror, reflecting and refocusing the light of others, in the process creating more and radiating it outward to warm and brighten the lives of those around us. In the giving, love grows. And so it expands, as the tiniest seed can mature into the tallest of trees.

In the midst of love, we find ourselves connected to all that came before and to all that could come after. We turn, seeing ourselves as drops within a stream that extends back to the beginning and forward to the end. And perhaps we will see that those limits are one, encompassing the love and life of infinity.

The Flower that Blooms Eternal

When the universe was naught but a seed
In the soil of blank emptiness,
Both within and beyond that point, which would lead
To the lives we dare now caress,
The flower you sow was already there,
Its power to grow beginning to share.

Opening slowly, ever holy,
Along the branches of time,
Blooming and reaching, always teaching,
Until all bells have ceased to chime,
When time is at an end,
Where all roads meet and spaces blend,
The point at which the universe
Has no more to amend,
This remains, with fully outstretched petals,
Multi-layered, multi-colored,
Enlivened, lit not by the sun,
Which eons will have smothered,
Expanding in another plane,
Where we can see it true, in spirit,
And in our lives it finds expression,
Leaves and vines extend,
To draw existence near it.

And so as we approach the end,
Reveal to us our part,
Reveal to us each piece of oneness,
In which a soul received its start.

Show, too, each spark's renewed uniqueness,
Freshly blossomed from the heart,
Reflecting back the love you lend,
Infused with new creative art.
Within us lie the atoms
Of the flower that blooms eternal,
From time before time, without beginning,
Immutable, immortal,
And in our hearts we feel the spark
As if our love were lit anew,
We understand, it always will expand:
For as we gave it, so it grew,
Touching all in you.

And so, a question lingers. What could be my specific contribution to this stream of all existence? What in particular might define the small but unique impact of my life? I realize it now. This is the question that has always been present, just beneath the surface.

Near the end of this past summer, I visited Grandma's old house. No one is living there now, since Grandma had been staying with my parents during the months since her stroke, and she has since moved into a nursing home. She has been wanting me to go up to her house for a while, so that I could look through Pop-Pop's old tools and pick out anything I wanted.

So, on an afternoon when my parents were out of town, I took Dad's truck and drove up the road to Grandma's house. After tossing a few fallen branches out of the driveway, I opened the garage, where Pop-Pop kept his tools and spent so many hours building beautiful wooden cabinets, tables, and other pieces of furniture. In the garage, I was greeted by the stuffiness of recent disuse and the faint, lingering aromas of wood shavings and oil. I began at the far end of the leftmost workbench and slowly made my way to the right. Along the way, I picked up various implements that had previously fit so familiarly into Pop-Pop's strong and weathered fingers. I had the distinct impression that, as I touched these tools and wooden surfaces, I was reaching back across the years to touch his hands.

By the end of my circuit through the garage, I found myself holding a few wrenches and screwdrivers, along with a small, black bubble level. Taking a slow, final look around this place where Pop-

Pop's presence and wisdom seemed so close at hand, I closed the garage door and walked out to the truck. As I deliberately paced out the distance from the house to the vehicle, I looked more closely at one of the wrenches in my hand, and I noticed that its end had been slightly but permanently twisted. The lines that should have run straight were warped into mild curves. What kind of torque had Pop-Pop applied to this piece of equipment to leave that lasting impact? What other marks had he made in his life? What parts of him, what parts of the love he shared, remain here with us today?

I thought back to this episode during the subsequent weekend, when I visited Grandma at the nursing home. We spoke about my upcoming move to Illinois, where I would be starting a doctoral program in environmental engineering. Thinking about my future, I couldn't help but also reflect on Grandma's past and present. Like Pop-Pop, she has made lasting impressions on the people and things around her. Even on that future day when she will close her eyes and find eternal rest, she will never leave us completely. Those impressions will endure.

Walking through the halls after wishing her a good night, I found myself wondering about what my own legacy might be. What are the marks that I will leave on the world after my life has passed me by? How do I touch the lives of those who come after? What parts of myself will echo down the years, cascading like the steps of a small waterfall and continuing on within the ever-flowing stream of existence? How much love will I leave behind?

If Today

If today is the final day
Upon this slanted, spinning sphere,
If tomorrow, songs of sorrow
Are lifted up by falling tear,
If you asked whether days gone past
Have shown a central, loving core,
Could I say mine did not decay?
Perhaps I'd not be sure.
Or,
If today be a normal day,
Let my love grow evermore.

POSTLUDE | THE LONGER ROAD

The Longer Road

The road through the woods is stranger
Than if you kept your spot,
Fraught with potential danger,
Filled with painful lot,
But still you may find you'll linger
Because you have been caught,
Not by a vicious finger,
But a peaceful thought.

The road can be full of wonder
If love and life are sought,
Not with a plan to plunder,
Only to be taught,
And so you'll return, no longer
The same to this same spot,
Longer your road, but stronger
You have now been wrought.

Love is the longer road. It is the way of connection, of relationship, of shared work and shared lives. It can be hard. It can be frustrating, even painful. It can lead to feelings of vulnerability. But it can also be fulfilling, illuminating, and strong. It can be full of wonder and awe. It can lead the way to peace.

As with anything, Peace Corps service is imperfect. But, at its core, I think it is based on the right ideas, ideas that are related to this longer road – integrating into a local community as much as possible, building relationships, exchanging ideas across cultures and borders. The individual experiences of Peace Corps Volunteers are extremely diverse and always unique, but, looking back on my own case in Uganda, I think it was nearly inevitable that my interactions with people and the natural world would cultivate and nurture the seeds of a greater love within my own heart. I am so fortunate to have had the experience that I did – to have met, developed friendships with, and come to love dedicated, caring, and understanding people. In some ways, my time in the Peace Corps was a long, slow awakening. It was a series of rebirths into a greater awareness of beauty, wonder, and love, which I hope will be sustained long into the future.

Unfortunately, it's also all too easy to talk negatively about development work, and not without cause. The work is not without its share of problems. Whether through corruption or mismanagement, funds do not always reach the intended beneficiaries. Products that do reach the correct people are not always locally appropriate, cost-effective, or environmentally conscious. They may not be easy to use and maintain, or they might undercut local people who make a living producing or selling similar items. To tug at the heartstrings of relatively affluent potential donors, some organizations continue to exploit the images of starving, apparently helpless children. This portrayal obviously does not fully capture the depth of experience of people living in these places, the complexities of their circumstances, and the fact that they can be – they must be – equal partners.

It remains too easy for people like me to view ourselves as saviors, as deliverers, as white knights riding in to rescue those in distress. It remains too easy for people like me to spend a few days in a faraway place, learn very little about the local context, do a little work that could have been done better by skilled people in that community, and return to our previous lives. It remains too easy for people like me to think we completely understand the lives of others whom we may have never met, and to believe that our straightforward solutions will work flawlessly and be universally admired by those "in need of help". It remains too easy for us to rush in confidently without understanding, to implement quick fixes without knowing the implications, perhaps out of some vague desire to "do good".

I've seen too many projects where this is the case. I've seen too many organizations fail to act responsibly, unwilling to change a flawed approach that is apparently set in stone. I've studied too many statistics exposing how many of our efforts fail, how many products are not used, and how many pieces of equipment fall into disrepair.

It is frustrating, infuriating, and sad. It's so easy to become jaded, cynical, and suspicious. It's also possible to go the other direction – to become numb to the concerns and the complexities, to take the shorter and quicker road of undemanding, unspecific, and inappropriate solutions. Heading in this direction, it can become easy to focus on output, rather than on outcome – on how much money is spent, on how many things are installed or distributed, rather than on how those things actually affect people's lives.

Surrounded by these manifold issues, it can be tempting to make the comprehensive statement that development simply does not work – that so much money has been spent and so much work has been attempted, while people all across the world continue to face difficult circumstances. It is easy to ask, "What do we have to show for our efforts?" There are opinions out there, many quite logically reasoned, that we should stop all of these attempts at development work, that we should step back and stand aside, letting the problems of the world figure themselves out. I can understand the line of thinking that leads to this point, but, despite the many poor examples of development work I have seen, it is not my view.

It is easy to talk negatively about development. The harder, but more important thing – once we acknowledge the obvious fact that this work is far from perfect – is to try to do it better. The truly valuable thing is to try to make it more impactful, less patronizing, more holistic, and more precise. Despite the setbacks, the difficulties, and the flaws, development work can still be good work. It can still be useful work, as long as it is done well, with careful attention and thoughtful reflection, and always with the goal of empowering members of the local community to take the lead.

When we simply stand apart and watch with disapproval on our lips, little is likely to change. We must keep working. We must keep pressing. We may make mistakes, we may need to change course, we may not consider everything, but we must keep trying to do better. Only then can we make true progress.

The Watcher

"I stand aside,
Out of reach I abide,
With nothing I'll ever collide,
Impartial observer, outside of the fervor,
The watcher, the impassive guide."

I heard that voice glide over what we have tried,
Over what all our struggles provide:
Ability, dignity, better agility
To face the next unforeseen tide.
I know it's imperfect, the work is still subject
To flaws and new pressures applied,
But I think we progress against chains that oppress
When together our souls forward stride,
Though the pains still refuse to subside.

I agree that the world is wide,
That we all must swallow our pride,
Objectively asking if work will be lasting
Or if, quickly, it will have died.
But the cold, steady "No" of that voice, like the crow
Who never will cease to deride,
Seems less than impartial, maintains the inertial,
Whose course, left un-countered, will slide.

None stands aside
Without letting the tide
Roll on as the evils abide.
So we all do decide, if not conscious, implied,
And change only comes from inside.

As I see it, this effort to do better work has two main aspects – the technical and the personal. Despite the tendency, especially among engineers, to focus on the technical, the personal is where everything must begin. It defines the entire enterprise. Fundamentally, development should be relational. Regardless of one's technical approach, at its core, the work should not be about "us" helping "them". It's easy to slip into this tired mantra, and it just doesn't work as well. It misses the longer road, which is always a two-way street. All who are involved teach and learn from one another. We all bring different sets of ideas and understandings to the table. If all can meet together on an equal footing, ready to be present, ready to listen and support, ready, if need be, to forgive, those ideas and perspectives can coalesce, creating something new that can benefit everyone.

True development is about all of us working together to create a more understanding, just, and peaceful world. It can only be accomplished through love and trust, by building relationships and by learning about others – their cultures, their belief systems, and their ways of seeing the universe. True development is about being open to seeing the world from a different perspective, and about realizing that those perspectives do not have to be antagonistic. Rather, they can complement one another.

True development is not something on a grand scale. It will not solve the world's problems in a day, a month, a year, or a decade. But, it might slowly help us all to develop into better people, one changed heart at a time. One day at a time, it might slowly help the world to develop into a better place, one that is more compassionate and understanding, one defined more and more by love and cooperation, rather than by hate and fear.

The relationship is primary. All else is secondary. The relationship paves the way for everything else. It is an effort that can begin and grow among those who are typically seen as unimportant, as the least, as the small. True power is there, in the fertile soil of connections defined by active and selfless love. From among the little blades of grass, far-reaching trees can emerge to touch the heavens.

One day, on a mildly warm afternoon in Uganda, I was sitting in a *matatu*, riding through Masaka on my way back to Kalisizo. The clouds and the sky on that day made the sun appear as a soft, red globe as it approached the horizon, and I could look straight at it without hurting my eyes. It looked calm and at peace, gently sending out the energy that fuels life on this planet. My mind turned to consider what is happening inside of that star, the chaos of atoms rocketing past and colliding with one another. Sometimes, they come together in such a way that they fuse to create something new and different, giving off huge amounts of energy in the process. It is a vastly complex dance, one that, perhaps, could act as a model for our own connected lives.

We are, all of us, works in progress, trying to do the best we can, but often falling short in our efforts. We don't always live up to the responsibility we have to one another. We don't always show the compassion and acceptance that should characterize our connectedness. Sometimes, we take steps in the wrong direction. Our efforts fail. Our grand ideas turn to dust. Our footsteps go astray. We see the diversity that characterizes a healthy community, and we mistake it as a source of division, conflict, and chaos. We see the differences of others as threats, rather than as opportunities for growth, understanding, and love.

But, through it all, we maintain our faith – our faith in one another, our faith in humanity, and our faith in the forces that pull us toward greater levels of relationship and community. We maintain our hope that, one day, the chaos will turn to cooperation, the hatred will turn to humility, the loathing will turn to love – that our discordant interactions will eventually coalesce to create something new, life-affirming, and beautiful.

The sun's light contains all the colors of the rainbow. Harmony cannot exist without a diversity of tone. We cannot fully exist without the relationships that link us one to another. They are the building blocks of life – the building blocks of love. They are the footprints we leave upon the longer road. Hidden in them lie the seeds of a new world, waiting to grow. Tend them well.

One Day

One day I tried to save the world,
To ascend the mountain, past cloud and fountain,
And look down upon creation,
To stand atop, my flag unfurled,
And stop the desperation.

One day I saw the issues clear,
With solutions solemn, perhaps each problem
Would desist its degradation,
And so would stop the fuel of fear
And end the exploitation.

One day I swam the starry sea,
Then sank back to earth, where a humble birth
Brings us all into our station.
As beads of dew on grass are we
When viewed with all creation.

But water the grass and let it grow
Until slow winds of change will blow,
For nothing will pass until we know
From where true love and hate both flow.

One day I searched my humble heart
To find you waiting, anticipating,
With knowing expectation,
To guide me true, to light my part
In life's grand orchestration.

True change falls not from mountain air,
Nor rains from clouds that wander there,
But rises from all the grasses where
Our many hearts one beat do share.

And you
And I who climbed so high,
Now reside where dewdrops lie
And try,
Through love and lowly rhyme,
To restore one heart, one day, one time.

AUTHOR'S NOTE

The contents of this book represent my own thoughts and ideas and do not reflect any position of the U.S. Government, the Peace Corps, or Brick by Brick. However, that is not to say those thoughts, or the work we did in Uganda, arose without the help and support of those organizations and institutions. They would not have been possible otherwise. I hesitate to list those who have contributed to the creation of this book and its ideas, for fear of forgetting someone. Suffice it to say, a multitude of family members, friends, and colleagues from different parts of the world have played a role in my life and in the path that led to the words contained in these pages, probably in more ways than I can know. I am forever grateful to all of them.

If you would like to learn about the work of Peace Corps Volunteers around the world, or if you are thinking about becoming a Peace Corps Volunteer, more information can be found on their website (www.peacecorps.gov).

If you are interested in supporting, participating in, or learning more about Brick by Brick's work, please visit their website (www.brickbybrick.org). Profits from the sale of this book will support the organization's continuing efforts to develop innovative solutions to the challenges faced by Ugandan communities through local engagement and partnership.

BIBLIOGRAPHY

Undoubtedly, the most important influences on the words I have written come from my personal interactions with friends and neighbors in Uganda, as well as with friends and family in the United States. A number of books also played a part in helping me to formulate some of the ideas contained within the preceding pages. Most of these titles were read while I was living in Uganda, although a few that I opened in the months after my Peace Corps service are also included. They are an eclectic group covering a wide range of topics. I list them here to acknowledge their contributions to my thoughts, and to encourage others to pick them up and take a look.

Achebe, Chinua. Things Fall Apart. First Anchor Books, 1954.

Arinze, Francis. Religions for Peace: A Call for Solidarity to the Religions of the World. Doubleday, New York, NY, 2002.

Bonaventure. The Soul's Journey into God, translated by Ewert Cousins. Paulist Press, New York, NY, 1978.

Bonhoeffer, Dietrich. A Testament to Freedom: The Essential Writings of Dietrich Bonhoeffer, edited by Geffrey B. Kelly and F. Burton Nelson. Harper One, New York, NY, 1995.

Bryson, Bill. A Short History of Nearly Everything. Broadway Books, New York, NY, 2003.

Cox, Brian and Jeff Forshaw. The Quantum Universe: (And Why Anything that Can Happen, Does). Da Capo Press, Boston, MA, 2011.

Diamond, Jared M. Guns, Germs, and Steel: The Fates of Human Societies. W.W. Norton & Company, Ltd., New York, NY, 1997.

Easterley, William. The White Man's Burden: Why the West's Efforts to Aid the Rest Have Done So Much Ill and So Little Good. Oxford Street Press, New York, NY, 2006.

Easwaran, Eknath. Your Life Is Your Message: Finding Harmony with Yourself, Others, and the Earth. Hyperion, New York, NY, 1992.

Epperly, Bruce G. Process Theology: A Guide for the Perplexed. T&T Clark, London, UK, 2011.

Esrey, Steven A., Jean Gough, Dave Rapaport, Ron Sawyer, Mayling Simpson-Hebert, Jorge Vargas, and Uno Winblad. Ecological Sanitation. Department for Natural Resources and the Environment, Swedish International Development Cooperation Agency, Stockholm, Sweden, 1998.

George, Rose. The Big Necessity: The Unmentionable World of Human Waste and Why It Matters. Holt Paperbacks, New York, NY, 2008.

Greene, Brian. The Elegant Universe: Superstrings, Hidden Dimensions, and the Quest for the Ultimate Theory. W.W. Norton & Company, Ltd., New York, NY, 2003.

Hartmann, Thom. The Last Hours of Ancient Sunlight: The Fate of the World and What We Can Do before It's Too Late. Three Rivers Press, New York, NY, 2004.

Hawking, Stephen, and Leonard Mlodinow. The Grand Design. Bantam Books, New York, NY, 2010.

Hesse, Hermann. Siddhartha. Project Gutenberg, 2008.

Ilibagiza, Immaculee, with Steve Erwin. Left to Tell: Discovering God amidst the Rwandan Holocaust. Hay House, Inc., Carlsbad, CA, 2006.

King, Martin Luther, Jr. A Testament of Hope: The Essential Writings and Speeches of Martin Luther King, Jr., edited by James M. Washington. Harper One, New York, NY, 1986.

Lane, Belden C. The Solace of Fierce Landscapes: Exploring Desert and Mountain Spirituality. Oxford University Press, New York, NY, 1998.

Lewis, C.S. Mere Christianity. Harper Collins, New York, NY, 2001.

Loewen, James. Lies My Teacher Told Me: Everything Your American History Textbook Got Wrong. Simon & Schuster, New York, NY, 2007.

Mihelcic, James R., Lauren M. Fry, Elizabeth A. Myre, Linda D. Phillips, and Brian D. Barkdoll. Field Guide to Environmental Engineering for Development Workers: Water, Sanitation, and Indoor Air. American Society of Civil Engineers (ASCE), 2009.

Moyo, Dambisa. Dead Aid: Why Aid Is Not Working and How There Is a Better Way for Africa. Farrar, Straus, and Giroux, New York, NY, 2010.

NEMA. State of the Environment Report for Uganda, 2010. National Environment Management Authority (NEMA), Kampala, 2010.

Nerburn, Kent. Small Graces: The Quiet Gifts of Everyday Life. MJF Books, New York, NY, 1998.

Obama, Barack. Dreams from My Father: A Story of Race and Inheritance. Three Rivers Press, New York, NY, 2004.

Pollack, Henry. A World without Ice. Penguin Group, New York, NY, 2009.

Rice, Andrew. The Teeth May Smile but the Heart Does Not Forget: Murder and Memory in Uganda. Picador, New York, NY, 2009.

Sachs, Jeffrey. The End of Poverty: Economic Possibilities for Our Time. Penguin Books, New York, NY, 2006.

Schumacher, E.F. Small is Beautiful: Economics as if People Mattered. Blond & Briggs, London, UK, 1973.

Shakespeare, William. The Sonnets. Avenel Books, New York, NY, 1961.

The Holy Bible, New International Version. Zondervan Corporation, Grand Rapids, MI, 1995.

The Upanishads, translated and commentated by Swami Paramananda from the original Sanskrit text. Halcyon Classics, Boston, MA, 1919.

Thoreau, Henry David. Walden. Running Press, Philadelphia, PA, 1990.

Thurow, Roger and Scott Kilman. Enough: Why the World's Poorest Starve in an Age of Plenty. PublicAffairs, New York, NY, 2009.

Tolstoy, Leo. The Kingdom of God is Within You, translated by Constance Garnett. Dover Publications, Inc. Mineola, NY, 2006.

Weil, Simone. Waiting for God, translated by Emma Craufurd. Harper Perennial, New York, NY, 2009.

Wessels, Tom. The Myth of Progress: Toward a Sustainable Future. University Press of New England, Lebanon, NH, 2013.

Zinn, Howard. A People's History of the United States: 1492 – 2001. Harper Perennial, New York, NY, 2003.

INDEX OF POEMS

For readers who would like to find particular poems, all poem titles are listed here in alphabetical order, along with corresponding page numbers.

ABOUT THE AUTHOR

John Trimmer was born in Harrisburg, Pennsylvania in 1987. After growing up in the rural, rolling hills of the southern part of the state, he attended Bucknell University in Lewisburg, Pennsylvania. He graduated in 2010 with a Bachelor of Science in Civil and Environmental Engineering. Moving to the University of South Florida, he enrolled in the Civil and Environmental Engineering Department's Peace Corps Master's International Program. From 2011 to 2014, he served as a United States Peace Corps Volunteer in Kalisizo, Uganda, where he worked with Brick by Brick Uganda, an organization focused on local education, economic development, and health. After concluding his service, John returned to the University of South Florida, where he graduated in 2015 with a Master of Science in Environmental Engineering. He is currently pursuing doctoral studies at the University of Illinois at Urbana-Champaign.

Made in the USA
San Bernardino, CA
11 February 2020